The
Politics of
Electoral Reform

4th edition

Michael Meadowcroft

BEECROFT PUBLICATIONS

2016

© Michael Meadowcroft

Published by:
Beecroft Publications
Waterloo Lodge
72 Waterloo Lane
Leeds LS13 2JF

www.beecroftpublications.co.uk

First published 1991, by Electoral Reform Society, with the support of Richard Wainwright
2nd edition 1997, published by Electoral Reform Society
3rd edition 2010, published by Beecroft Publications, revised 2012
4th edition 2016 published with the support of the Andrew Wainwright Trust, which, with the Scurrah Wainwright Charitable Trust, work for political and social reform and tackling the root cause of poverty respectively. Website: www. wainwrighttrusts.org.uk

ISBN 978-0-9930909-3-6

Design and typography by Elizabeth Bee (c) 2016

Printed and bound in Great Britain by 4edge Ltd, Essex

CONTENTS

GLOSSARY

Abbreviations used in this book:

AMS   Alternative Member System

AV   Alternative Vote

AV+   Alternative Vote Plus

FPTP   First-Past-The-Post

PR   Proportional Representation

STV   Single Transferable Vote

THE POLITICS OF ELECTORAL REFORM

R ECENT LITERATURE ON ELECTORAL REFORM, and the considerable media interest in the subject, particularly at the time of the 2011 UK referendum on the Alternative Vote, have tended to concentrate on electoral arithmetic and on party proportionality. The electoral lottery of the 2015 general election has widened the debate to bring forward issues of legitimacy.

In this revised edition of *The Politics of Electoral Reform* Michael Meadowcroft examines the wider implications of changing the Westminster voting system, not least its role in combatting the increasing disillusion in our political processes. In particular, he sets out the political consequences of different electoral systems. From his experience as a member of parliament he also examines the mythical advantages claimed for the single member constituency.

THE AUTHOR

Michael Meadowcroft has been active in politics since 1958, holding professional and national offices within the Liberal party. He served as an elected city and metropolitan county councillor in Leeds for 15 years and was Liberal MP for Leeds West, 1983-87. He has an MPhil degree in Leeds political history and was a senior visiting fellow at the Policy Studies Institute in 1989. He chaired the  Electoral Reform Society from 1989 to 1993 and was a member of its governing council for many years.

Over the past 25 years he has worked as a consultant to new and emerging democracies. He has also worked as a journalist and writer and much of his writing is archived on the website: www.bramley. demon.co.uk

PREFACE

THE 2015 GENERAL ELECTION WAS rightly called 'the lottery election' with its outcome in suspense until the close of the polls, depending on the capricious spread of votes amongst six parties all polling more than one million votes. It was the most disproportionate election ever in terms of party seats gained for votes cast.[1] The Conservative party won an overall majority of six seats on just 37 per cent of the vote – in other words approaching two out of three electors voted against the party which now forms a government. The election saw travesties of individual constituency results, including for the first time an MP elected with less than a quarter of the votes cast.[2] First-Past-the-Post (FPTP) voting was never satisfactory when there were only two parties. Indeed, in 1951, when the two major parties between them secured more than 94 per cent of the vote, the Conservative party won a majority in the House of Commons even though the Labour party had most votes. Now, with five significant parties across the whole country, plus the two nationalist parties in Scotland and Wales, it is simply not fit for purpose.

If the seats in parliament do not reflect to a significant extent how the electorate votes, what is the point of holding elections? The result

---

1   For this and other statistics on this election see Jess Garland & Chris Terry, *The 2015 General Election - A Voting System in Crisis*, Electoral Reform Society, June 2015.
2   Dr Alasdair McDonnell, SDLP, Belfast South.

of the 2015 election is so unrepresentative of the votes cast that the government's legitimacy has to be seriously questioned. What claim to any mandate to govern can a party have that secured 11.3 million votes but which had 18.4 million votes cast against it?

The uncertain outcome of the election was even more remarkable when one realises that, despite the multiparty 'lottery', more than half the seats are safe for one party or another. Indeed, four weeks before polling day the Electoral Reform Society declared the winner in 368 of the 650 seats.[3] All but five were predicted accurately, comprising more than 25 million voters. These electors doggedly, but perhaps quixotically, carried on voting even though their votes were going to have no effect on the result. Today extremely skilful computer programmes can identify swing voters in marginal seats. Consequently, those living in safe constituencies will be lucky to hear from any candidate, whereas the handful of voters targeted in marginal seats will be overwhelmed by a deluge of literature, letters and telephone calls. This is a travesty of the democratic process.

At this election, as at other recent ones, efforts were made to circumvent the failings of the electoral system by codifying tactical voting to encourage electors to abandon their preferred choice in order to try to prevent the election of the candidate or party that they least favour. It is surely bizarre that we put up with an electoral system that requires such methods to ameliorate its faults.

The turnout at the 2015 election was slightly higher in Scotland than in 2010, probably as a consequence of the Scottish National party's (SNP) momentum and the heightened political involvement at the referendum on Scottish independence. However, in the rest of the United Kingdom it was the same as in 2010; in other words one third of the electorate did not vote. The legitimacy of the Conservative government is further undermined by the fact that its candidates secured the votes of fewer than one quarter of the electorate. Even this

3   www.electoral-reform.org.uk/blog/reading-tea-leaves. Also published in *Daily Mail*, 10 April 2015.

figure is exaggerated by the failure of the registration system to enrol more than an estimated 85 per cent of the eligible voters. The change to individual registration, relying on each eligible elector registering himself or herself, as opposed to household registration, under which the head of the household is responsible for the registration of all members of that household, is thought to have reduced the numbers on the register by some 10 per cent. It particularly hit certain sections of the population, younger voters, those in poorer areas and, most markedly, students who in the past had all been registered by the university if they lived in university accommodation. This is a classic case of principle versus effectiveness. Personally, I would have kept to the pragmatic benefits of household registration in order to maximise the numbers on the register.

The party most detrimentally affected by the vagaries of the FPTP electoral system was the United Kingdom Independence party (UKIP), which won just a single seat despite polling 3.9 million votes. I suspect that many politicians who are strongly opposed to UKIP's politics quietly acquiesce to this injustice. I believe that UKIP, with its excessive nationalism and negativity towards so much of the political agenda, is a dangerous party but, nevertheless, I cannot justify a system that fiddles them out of their legitimate representation.

Extremism has to be combatted by argument and persuasion and not by electoral sleight of hand. Quite apart from the moral argument for fairness, making a party and its candidates into electoral martyrs is counter-productive. Take the example of France where the far right Front National (FN) polled just 0.3 per cent at the 1973 parliamentary elections; but by 1986 it polled 9.8 per cent and won 35 seats under proportional representation (PR). The French mainstream parties took fright and abandoned PR so that two years later the FN won no seats at all, despite winning the same level of support. All that happened thereafter was that the FN's support increased – to 12.7 per cent in 1993 and 15.3 per cent in 1997. Internal problems reduced its support in 2002 and 2007 but in 2012 its presidential candidate polled 17.9

per cent and in 2014 it gained control of 11 municipal councils. Manipulating the electoral system against the party, rather than relying on argument and persuasion, simply enhanced its support.

How long will UKIP's voters, and for that matter the supporters of other parties cheated by the system, complain bitterly but acquiesce peacefully to the electoral conspiracy on the part of the two major parties? The lack of legitimacy of the winner increases election by election. Will those cheated by it put up with the lack of representative democracy indefinitely? I doubt it.

Arguably the ability of UKIP to present itself as the representative of those marginalised by the establishment and its mainstream parties over many years contributed to the high vote for "Leave" amongst these voters in the referendum on membership of the European Union on 23 June 2016. None of the parties with influence within Westminster have confronted the legitimate concerns of those whose jobs in heavy industry have been largely swept away by globalisation and by undercutting on prices, and consequently UKIP – and the Leave campaign – were able to play on their genuine fears without any possibility of accountability. Polly Toynbee made the point well:

> ... our electoral system blocks the birth of new parties. The seething anti-Westminster wrath must partly spring from 4 million UKIP voters granted just one MP. If UKIP had its fair share of MPs, sunlight would have exposed that quarrelsome ragbag of often nasty eccentrics, just as [Margaret] Hodge saw off Barking's 12 chaotic BNP councillors. Denying those voters a voice helps explain why those anti-EU, anti-foreigner emotions erupted so disastrously on Thursday.[4]

In the end nothing is gained by using a defective electoral system to avoid tackling serious issues, however unpalatable.

---

4   Opinion column. *The Guardian*, 25 June 2016. Margaret Hodge has been the Labour MP for Barking since 1994.

The most important challenge to the two major United Kingdom parties' attitude to the electoral system arises from their almost complete wipeout in Scotland under FPTP.[5] First, what conceivable reason can there be for their own self-interest in retaining the existing electoral system? To do so is electoral masochism of a high order. The SNP, with precisely 50 per cent of the vote, won 56 of the 59 seats, whilst Labour with 24 per cent and the Conservatives with 15 per cent were reduced to one MP each. In the forseeable political future there is little prospect of there being a significant change in such blatant misrepresentation. Do the two parties really wish to continue their suffering and to deny Scottish citizens what they presumably believe are the advantages of Labour and Conservative representation?

Second, however, there is an even greater issue of principle: are these two unionist parties, now virtually unrepresented in Scotland, prepared to impose legislation on the citizens of Scotland on all the issues not devolved to the Scottish Parliament, in effect by the votes of English MPs alone? Whatever the issues or the policies, this parliamentary arithmetic produces a can't lose situation for the SNP who can now blame the UK government, without Scottish involvement, for every unpopular decision.

UK prime ministers must consider whether they are prepared to put the union at risk simply because they are not prepared to envisage a change to an electoral system that will produce a more representative and accountable forum for debate and decision on key issues.

To its credit the SNP is officially in favour of the introduction of the Single Transferable Vote (STV) and it restated this following the 2015 election, even in the knowledge that it would bring the loss of a number of SNP seats.[6]

---

5   The Liberal Democrats were also reduced to a single MP but they are officially in favour of a change to the Single Transferable Vote.
6   John Swinney MSP, Deputy First Minister of Scotland, BBC *Question Time*, 8 May 2015.

It is against the background of the consequences of the 2015 general election that this fourth edition of this booklet has been written. It deliberately goes beyond the superficial arithmetic and dangers of party proportionality and seeks to look at the wider problems of enhancing our flagging democracy and to improving the health of our politics. It is published as a contribution to the debate on how best our politics can connect with the electorate and how our democratic structure is equipped to cope with all the stresses and strains currently placed on it.

Other publications on electoral systems have tended to concentrate on academic considerations or on arithmetical outcomes. This booklet looks at the political arguments in the hope of bringing the debate into the mainstream of public and political discussion.

INTRODUCTION

IT WAS THROUGH GRITTED TEETH that many supporters of electoral reform, myself included, backed the case for the Alternative Vote at a referendum in May 2011. It was a very tentative small step away from voting with an 'X' and would have been a way of 'officially' enabling tactical voting but, in Liberal MP Nick Clegg's words, it was in essence a 'miserable little compromise'[1] which was much too easy to defeat. The scale of the referendum vote, two to one against change, was thought by many commentators to have taken electoral reform off the political agenda for a generation,[2] but we have seen yet again the truth of former prime minister Harold Macmillan's adage of what affects politics most, 'Events, dear boy, events.'[3]

It was the events in the latter part of the 2010 parliament, with the rise of UKIP and the increase in the electoral support for the SNP increasing the threat to the two party hegemony, that have put electoral reform firmly back on to the agenda.[4] The results of the 2015

1   *The Independent,* 22 April 2010.
2   See, for instance, Vernon Bogdanor, 'This general election will be fought along regional lines', *Financial Times,* 4 January 2015, and also Mark D'Arcy, Parliamentary Correspondent, on the BBC website: www.bbc.co.uk/news/uk-politics-13311252.
3   Iain Dale, *The Dictionary of Conservative Quotations,* Biteback, 2013, p262.
4   See, for instance, *New Statesman,* 16 December 2012 and 14 February 2014, and Susanna Rustin in *The Guardian,* 8 May 2013.

general election and the lottery of its outcome, thanks to First-Past-the-Post (FPTP), have alarmed all those concerned for the future of democracy in Britain.[5]

One significant advance in the electoral reform debate is that it is not as dominated by the issue of fairness to minor parties, or of representing national parties proportionately in parliament, legitimate though such arguments are, but by a growing acceptance that the nature of the electoral system has a role to play in reviving the health of our democratic process.[6]

Faced still with the deepest economic crisis for 75 years, and a global ecological imperative, it is more vital than ever for citizens to have confidence in the capacity of their politicians to create a viable and humane future.

Under the FPTP plurality system we have seen an increasing level of adversarial politics, with the infantilist slanging match of Prime Minister's Questions, an increasingly negative style of party propaganda, the increasing reliance on appeals to tactical voting, particularly by the Liberal Democrats, and an almost complete absence of cross-party public meetings. There is, in 2016, little public political debate, particularly in urban areas, only the media-staged question sessions and the increasing use of social media. No wonder that voting at general elections now hovers around the 60 per cent mark and that the current membership of all the political parties combined – even with the recent surge of Labour

---

5   For statistics on this election see Jess Garland & Chris Terry, *The 2015 General Election - A Voting System in Crisis,* Electoral Reform Society, June 2015. For a record of the capricious and superficial nature of the electoral process, see Nick Robinson, *Election Notebook*, Bantam Press, 2015.
6   Dennis Kavanagh and David Butler, *The British General Election of 2005*, Palgrave Macmillan, 2005, pp249-253. See also the Report of the Select Committee report on Voter Disengagement in the United Kingdom, http://www.parliament.uk/voter-engagement-in-the-uk, in particular the section on Electoral Reform in section 7, and the many submissions on this topic published by the Committee.

membership during its leadership election – is less than that of the Church of England.

If this long systemic decline of British politics were not enough, we had the abuse of parliamentary expenses by significant numbers of MPs and Peers. The exposure, in 2009, of some members of parliament who manipulated their different addresses to maximise their expenses claims and to minimise their capital gains tax liability, with some even claiming for mortgages already paid off, wrongly tarred all MPs with a deeply damaging brush. Those MPs who have behaved honourably may well be able to re-gild their image, but the voters' understandable attitude was vividly summed up by a television clip of one elector who 'wanted to be able to vote against her MP without voting against her party.'[7] Only a preferential voting system, specifically the Single Transferable Vote (STV) – under which, in a multi-member constituency, the elector numbers his or her preferences – can enable an elector to make this distinction, as we shall see below.

The present crisis has catalysed a willingness to consider proportional representation, on the part of politicians, party officers and celebrities as a means of restoring some confidence in British democracy. This is all to the good, but it begs the question of what is meant by PR. The general lack of awareness about electoral reform and the consequences of different systems is manifest – and alarming. Some electoral systems, by putting even more power into the hands of the party machines, would actually make the situation worse. Hence it is important to look at the implications of the main alternatives, particularly if the electorate is to be asked to demonstrate its opinion at a referendum.

Electoral reform is the final major democratic change required to establish an effective and accountable democratic process in the United Kingdom. When, certainly in the forseeable future, it has been instituted, it will, like all other changes, soon become embedded

7   Un-named elector on BBC *Newsnight* programme on Julie Kilbride, 28 May 2009

as it has been elsewhere. It has always been the way with reforms, and people will wonder what all the fuss was about. It has never been otherwise: titanic struggles to withstand change, eventually overcome, followed by legislation and subsequent acceptance. Is there a single voice now saying that to be a voter one must have a property qualification? Who now argues for the secret ballot to be abandoned? Who would dare even to suggest taking the vote away from women? Does anyone now believe that a candidate's party should be forbidden to appear on the ballot paper? Is it thought that 18 to 21-year-olds are intrinsically less responsible when exercising their votes? All these were keenly fought reforms in their day which are now embedded and accepted.

Our election processes have been amended piecemeal over the past 170 years and we have this one further major change still to make. A simple plurality system may well have been just about adequate before the advent of nationally organised political parties in the 1870s, but it is a heavier and heavier millstone around the neck of a faltering political system that has to cope with the pressures of the 21st century.

Of course it is important that the party topping the poll wins the election – unlike 1951 and February 1974 under FPTP – and it is important that parties, large and small, are treated fairly, but there is today an increasing awareness that our democracy is incapable of coping with the complexities and challenges of the current political agenda. Coupled with this concern is a growing frustration with the superficiality of political debate in Britain and with the lack of individual involvement in the political process. The public's cynicism about politicians and parties generally may or may not be justified – but it is extremely dangerous.

DEMOCRACY & ELECTIONS

ELECTION OR SELECTION?

UNDER BRITAIN'S PRESENT FPTP ELECTORAL system there is a positive disincentive to grapple with issues and to apply even a modicum of intellectual rigour to the resolution of problems. A small switch of votes on an unpopular issue can put a swathe of MPs out of parliament, whilst a failure to toe the party line, however unrealistic that line might be, brings the risk of deselection. The highly sophisticated computer programmes that can now identify the relatively few potential 'switch' voters in the minority of seats that are not safe, enable parties to concentrate resources on these individual voters, and to ignore everyone else. This travesty of the democratic process is only possible with FPTP.

The Liberal Democrats resort to a particular tactic that is in essence equally strategic rather than political. Under FPTP they have somehow to break into the two-party closed shop. The only way that they can achieve this is to play on the inherently greater local dislike for one or other party as opposed to the Liberal Democrats. So in constituency after constituency, the Liberal Democrats run the 'two horse race' argument – 'only the Lib Dem can beat Labour/Conservative here, so, to avoid letting Labour/Conservative in, you must vote Liberal Democrat'. In most constituencies there is no objective evidence for the argument, but it can still be run in the hope of creating a swing which will be self-fulfilling. Whether the Liberal Democrats really wish to conduct their politics in this recondite and simplistic fashion I know not, but as long as we have FPTP, with all its iniquities, they can hardly be blamed for resorting to any tactic that gives them an opportunity to overcome its inherent bias.

In 2015, after five years in coalition government, the Liberal Democrats tried to use the tactical voting ploy. In fact their increasing emphasis, as the election approached, on differentiation from their Conservative partners in government was an indication of their intentions for an election strategy. It was, I suppose, worth trying even though it ultimately failed miserably to prevent their abject electoral failure. In addition, the electoral appeal of UKIP and the strength of the SNP north of the border, and of the Green party in a number of constituencies, inevitably increased a recourse to negative, tactical campaigning in an attempt to minimise the detrimental voting effect on the two main parties of electors being tempted to support the minor parties as a way of showing their disaffection for traditional politics.

Neither the concentration on the handful of swing voters nor the obsession with tactical voting is healthy politics, but both are a direct consequence of the FPTP voting system. Politics is about power, and political parties are in the business of winning power. Of course they are guilty as charged of the offence of aiding and abetting the increasing – and dangerously accelerating – ill-health of UK politics. While all those concerned for the future should continue to appeal to politicians' better natures, it would be much easier to enforce a change in the electoral system which would make it pointless for them to continue these facile and simplistic tactics.

The reality remains that for as long as we have FPTP, then in a majority of constituencies it is the party, and not the electors, that selects the MP, in that, even if they heartily dislike the selected candidate, the voters are sufficiently loyal to the party to swallow hard and vote for him or her. Even in the lottery election of 2015 this was true in 363 constituencies. In recent years, rather than being sensitive to this excess of party power, the parties have exercised it to a greater extent than hitherto. Within the context of the 2009 exposures of the manipulation of parliamentary allowances by some MPs in that parliament, the then prime minister, David Cameron, made it clear that attempts by Conservative MPs to challenge the assessment of the Independent Parliamentary Standards Authority (IPSA) would not be tolerated and a number of members were deselected or retired, apparently under duress,[1] while Labour established a 'star chamber' which also denied a number of sitting MPs the opportunity to stand for re-election.[2] However, such centralised action is not a new phenomenon and there have been a number of extreme examples over recent years.

Historically the Labour Party National Executive Committee (NEC) has taken the authority to intervene in the selection of by-election candidates. One blatant example occurred in 1991 in Hemsworth, one of its safest seats, when Ken Capstick, a former miners' leader, secured by far the highest number of nominations towards selection as the official candidate. However, Labour's NEC stepped in, excluded him even from the shortlist for interview, and appointed Derek Enright as the candidate.[3] As would rightly be assumed, Messrs Capstick and Enright were from opposite ends of the party's ideological spectrum.[4] Ironically earlier, in 1984, when a more left-wing element was in the ascendancy in the party, Derek Enright was the retiring Labour MEP for Leeds and was himself deselected! In neither case did the electors have any say in the type of Labour candidate they could vote for. As in all single-member seats, it is a party list of one, take it or leave it. The Labour NEC's powers over candidate selection can also now be

---

1   *Daily Telegraph,* re 'ethical pledge', 18 May 2009, and action re Anthony Steen, 22 May 2009.
2   *Daily Telegraph,* 27 May 2009 - the first four victims were Margaret Moran, Elliot Morley, Dr Ian Gibson and David Chaytor.
3   Ken Capstick later abandoned the Labour party and from 1996 fought four somewhat quixotic elections for the Socialist Labour party led by Arthur Scargill.
4   Andy Smith, *Faces of Labour,* Verso, 1996, p130.

imposed in relation to general elections. For instance, the present Labour MP for Leeds North East, Fabian Hamilton, only became the party's candidate there in 1997 because the NEC refused to accept the locally democratically selected, and more left-wing, Liz Davies as Labour candidate.[5]

The powers of the 'selectorate' rather than the electorate bring the unedifying spectacle of prospective candidates touting themselves around the country, boning up on the problems of towns and villages they may never see again, in order to impress the party elite in constituency after constituency. A seat with the best prospects, where the party is strongest, may be geographically and in character far distant from their experience. Eventual adoption by a local party in effect presents the party voter at the subsequent election with no choice. Nor must it be thought that safe seats necessarily have a high level of party membership: often, through complacency and the very fact of the election itself being a foregone conclusion, party membership is minuscule. For instance, in her Salford Labour party fief, the then MP Hazel Blears, following allegations of misuse of parliamentary allowances, had to face a motion of no confidence. Even given such a hot topic, only 51 party members were present to vote for her to keep her seat – by 37 to 14.[6]

A contributory factor to Labour's near demise in Scotland in the 2015 election was its long complacency in many of its so-called safe seats, where party membership and organisation were at a disastrously low level, and tailor-made for the SNP incursions. Jeremy Corbyn's success at the Labour leadership election in summer 2015 was aided by the significant increase in party membership (and in registered supporters) he catalysed, on top of the very low base.

In 2013 in Falkirk, which at least until then had been a safe Labour seat, the opportunity arose to select a new Labour candidate for the 2015 general election. The sitting MP, Eric Joyce, had resigned from

5 See http://en.wikipedia.org/wiki/Liz_Davies
6 *The Guardian*, 18 June 2009.

the Labour party and announced that he would not be contesting the forthcoming election, following a conviction for assault. The local Labour party then embarked on a tortuous selection process under which the Unite union recruited multiple members and paid their initial party subscriptions in order to secure the nomination of its preferred candidate. This caused uproar and a number of high level resignations and suspensions, and eventually led to legal action. The problem with the FPTP election system is that loyal Labour supporting voters at the subsequent election have no choice but to vote for whichever candidate emerges from such a flawed process.[7]

In February 2014 two Conservative MPs in safe constituencies, Anne McIntosh in Thirsk and Malton, and Tim Yeo in South Suffolk, were deselected by their local associations. At the 2010 general election both had been warmly recommended to the voters by the Conservatives and enough voters duly followed the advice to elect them comfortably. Four years later, and without any reference to those selfsame voters, they were adjudged unfit to be recommended again. In both cases they had simply fallen out with their local Conservative associations, allegedly on political grounds. In 2015 the electors in both constituencies duly voted for the replacement Conservative candidates. Under FPTP, a change of opinion on the key issue of the acceptability of the member of parliament within the relatively small 'selectorate' of the party membership effectively prevents the voters from making that decision.[8]

Ferdinand Mount, one time advisor to Mrs Thatcher, suggests that, for Labour, the problem is often founded in financial sponsorship:

> Labour MPs would be sponsored by one or more of the trade unions which were strongly represented in local factories and offices. The Islington North constituency, for example, was in the gift of the Transport and General Workers Union, which dominated

7   *The Guardian,* 22 November 2013.
8   *Yorkshire Post,* 1 February 2014 and *The Guardian,* 4 February 2014.

the Archway bus depot. The constituency also had a strong Irish flavour, so that a bus driver of Irish descent was a shoo in.[9]

Essex university professor Anthony King's 2015 book makes a further point about the increasing dangers of party members determining candidates:

> A more intractable problem concerns the exaggerated role that party members and activists play in the affairs of the British state.... [A]lthough there are occasional up-ticks in the parties' enrolment of new members, especially among smaller parties such as the Scottish National party and UKIP, the long-term trend among political parties as a whole is downward, with their aggregate memberships today numbered in the few hundreds of thousands rather than the millions of yesteryear. Yet those tiny bands of party members have far more lethal political weaponry in their hands than they ever did before. Not only do they continue to select parliamentary candidates (and, in effect, elect the local MP in a majority of parliamentary constituencies), but they now elect the leaders of their parties – that is, decide which two or three people will be in a position to become prime minister. They absolutely determine the choice of prime minister offered to the people.[10]

A recent innovation from the Conservative leadership has been the 'open' primary under which all voters in a constituency are permitted to vote as between different party nominees. Using this process, Dr Sarah Wollaston was chosen as the Conservative candidate for Totnes in August 2009 in a poll of more than 12,000. On the face of it this is a commendable idea, however it undermines still further the case for the political party. As Ferdinand Mount states:

9   Ferdinand Mount, *The New Few*, Simon & Schuster, 2012, p132.
10 Anthony King, *Who Governs Britain?*, Pelican, 2015.

... of course, if widely adopted, the open primary would be another nail in the coffin of the mass political party. Why bother to subscribe, let alone canvass or attend meetings, if any old resident can blow in and usurp the most cherished right of the local party, to select its candidate for the House of Commons?[11]

Of course, this is yet again a problem of the single member constituency. With STV in multi-member constituencies, the elector has the opportunity to express his or her preferences between different candidates nominated by the party.

If, under FPTP, a constituency is not a safe seat we then move into the realms of tactical voting. Slogans such as 'Don't waste your vote' or 'Don't let Labour/ the Tories in,' plus gimcrack opinion polls designed to bolster party claims of being ahead, are the present stuff of election campaigning in such seats. There are now even organisations dedicated to tactical voting, simply because the electoral system actively discourages a positive choice and puts a premium on negative voting. Why should an elector have to vote for a party or a candidate other than his or her first choice just to keep out a party or an individual they are keen to see defeated? Surely a system is much better in which electors can rank their preferences in order with very little chance of their vote being 'wasted'.

Arguably an even worse trait of our current politics is the slanging match aimed at undermining the credibility of one's opponents, on the basis that putting voters off completely may assist the incumbent party or candidate and, in any case, the 'Buggins' Turn' principle means that one day the positions are bound to be reversed. The consequent damage to the health of our democracy generally is not even considered. Alas, there is a Gresham's Law in politics as in economics: bad politics drives out good and our electoral system allows the perpetrators to get away with it, debasing the political coinage at virtually no electoral risk to themselves. Prime Minister's Questions

11 Ferdinand Mount, op cit p142.

each Wednesday in parliament are a travesty of parliamentary practice and the contest has reduced politics to a point scoring slanging match which undermines public respect even more. The advent of Jeremy Corbyn to the Labour leadership has mitigated this to some extent but it still often reverts to type. What is the gain of being elected to an office which is held in contempt by a majority of the public? We have to re-establish respect for parliament and its members. Towards this, we need an electoral system in which parties and candidates benefit from support from the later preferences of supporters of other parties and candidates, thus discouraging negative tactics, in order to maximise their own success.

STRONG GOVERNMENT OR EFFECTIVE GOVERNMENT?

The present system does not even bring effective government. It may often bring strong government, in the sense that a single party government given a working majority in the House of Commons can usually whip its supporters through the lobby to pass legislation. Even the coalition government formed after the 2010 election had to resort to new rules, for instance in relation to a fixed-term parliament, to underpin its survival. But to what end if what is passed does not find a resonance amongst the public and if the art of persuasion and debate is perceived as neither worthwhile in principle nor possible in practice? The politician's version of the old adjunct in the preacher's notes, 'argument weak, bang the pulpit', is to say it was a 'manifesto promise' as if this were some kind of magical talisman able to overwhelm all rational opposition.

The appeal to a 'manifesto promise' is, of course, used selectively and discarded when it suits the party, such as Labour's 1997 election manifesto promise to hold a referendum on electoral reform. It is inapplicable to huge unanticipated issues, such as the invasion of Iraq, but, above all, it is in itself an arithmetical nonsense. No government in over seventy years has had a majority of votes cast, let alone a majority of the electorate. At the 2005 election, Tony Blair's Labour party secured only a miserable 23.5 per cent of the electorate's support. Five years later, David Cameron's Conservative party secured just 1 per cent more. How in such circumstances can a government claim to have any effective mandate to govern? Mrs Thatcher's nemesis, the poll tax, provided a classic example: strong government enabled it to be passed through parliament; ineffective government meant that it could not be sustained against the weight of public opposition. Ironically the formation of the coalition government after the last election required a joint agreement, which superseded both parties' manifestos, even though much of its content was drawn from them. Even then some of the issues which proved most contentious for the Liberal Democrats, such as NHS reform, were in neither party's manifesto nor in the coalition agreement.

Thus we have the appearance of effective government but not its reality. The determination to maintain the fiction, and self-deception, of strong government is nowhere more vividly seen than in the ritual finger-pointing at the iniquities of poor benighted countries that have proportional representation. Even leaving aside for the moment the fact that few such countries have a PR system that would match the criteria laid down to general approval in 1997 for the Jenkins Commission on Electoral Systems,[12] the fact is that a country such as Sweden that is highly regarded as being democratic and well run, does, of course, elect its governments by PR. It always used to be Italy, with its supposedly frequent and capricious changes in government, that was held up as the nightmare example to frighten British voters. The fact that its governmental changes usually turned out to be minor re-shuffles and that its underlying problem was a lack of any significant political change were conveniently ignored. By comparison, studies show that British cabinet ministers are reshuffled more often – under both Labour and Conservative administrations – than in most other European

---

12 See 'Terms of Reference and Membership', in *The Report of the Independent Commission on the Voting System*, Cm 4090-1, October 1998, page v.

governments where ministers are in post for an average of two and a half years. In addition, fewer British ministers are appointed who have expertise in the subject matter covered by their departments.[13]

For some time the public has had a declining sense of respect for its politicians, partly because they seem remote from its concerns, partly because they seem impotent when faced with today's complex problems and partly because the public sense that, in order to stay in office, they were not telling them the whole truth. The public exposure, in 2009, of a number of MPs abusing their parliamentary allowances accelerated the decline. It will take time to recover respect and esteem for MPs. The public are not fools and the situation will certainly not be helped by politicians clinging to FPTP and proclaiming its supposed virtues like a current version of the emperor's new clothes, in which fiction is presented as fact with the public being increasingly and instinctively aware that it simply is not so.

Power for its own sake is seen as less and less attractive if it has to depend on an electoral lottery one day delivering the jackpot. Former Labour MP and cabinet minister Clare Short was one of the few MPs from the major parties to stand up for even-handedness and she sat out the remaining months of the 2005 parliament as an independent MP dedicated to achieving electoral reform. She has a long track record of honesty on the subject. She told her party conference:

> I cannot in all fairness argue that it is wrong for Mrs Thatcher to implement her legislation on a minority vote but then argue that it would be right for Labour to do the same.[14]

Clare Short's forthrightness is highly relevant given that the 2005 Labour government had less than 35 per cent of the votes cast. It is the open acceptance of this plain unvarnished principle that opens

---

13 Hugh Cleary and Richard Reeves, *The culture of 'churn' and the price we all pay,* Demos, 2009.
14 Labour party conference, 1989.

up the debate. It ensures that electoral reform is seen as a key way of raising the level of political debate and of enabling the country to cope effectively with the very real problems that face it individually and collectively. Decisions about such emotive and important principles as democracy and government can never be entirely objective but at least subjectivity can be minimised by the open acceptance that all parties need to judge each other by the same standards.

KEY CRITERIA

Election systems are not value free. Their diverse characteristics influence different aspects of the democratic process. Politicians may well want an electoral system to deliver a host of different aims, but there are three key democratic objectives by which a representative voting system should be judged:

- **accountability:** elected representatives should be collectively and individually responsible to the voters;
- **equal value of votes:** the value of the individual vote should not be distorted by factors such as geography and class and the number of 'wasted' votes should be kept to a minimum;
- **effective choice:** voters should be offered as wide a choice as practicable between parties and candidates, towards the formation of an effective government.

STUMBLING BLOCKS

There are currently just two major stumbling blocks in the way of change, which must be cleared before these key criteria can be applied to the different systems.

The first is the weight of vested interests coupled with the recent relative docility of the British public. Not surprisingly, those elected under the present FPTP system have tended to favour it. Any system that elected them, and, in particular, provided safe seats for a majority of them, was by definition an excellent system. They relied on the apparent fact that a vast and sustained public uprising akin to the

Chartists or the suffragettes, was unlikely to spring up even though there was ample polling evidence that the public favoured change and would back an electoral reform bill. Of course when MPs are legislating for how other bodies should be elected they impose a variety of other systems but never FPTP – whether in Scotland, Wales and Northern Ireland, for European MEPs and even for the mayor of London – but never for themselves.[15]

Similarly, of course, MPs would never conceive of using FPTP for their own internal elections. The Speaker of the House of Commons is elected by an exhaustive ballot of MPs in which, until a candidate has over 50 per cent, the bottom candidate is excluded and MPs vote again to choose between the remaining candidates – ie by transferable votes.

Equally, all three main parties elect their leaders by one form or another of transferable ballot. Church of England Bishop Colin Buchanan points out:

> There would not be so much horror as incredulity if anyone proposed that either [Labour or Conservative] party should allow any number of nominations for leader, and would then accept as leader the one who received the most votes on a single snap ballot. This procedure would of course be 'simple', *but simplicity will not suffice when MPs are themselves the electors.*[16]

Even more marked will be the situation for Labour at the next general election, whether or not the party parts company with Jeremy Corbyn as its leader. The struggle within the parliamentary party and amongst the party members is so acute that neither the Left who elected Corbyn nor the rest of the party which opposed him, can comfortably be contained within a single Labour party under FPTP,

15 Colin Buchanan, *Christian Ethics and Electoral Reform,* Grove Books, 2015, p8.
16 Buchanan ibid, p8, emphasis in original.

which requires one agreed candidate in each constituency. Even worse would be a list PR system which would produce an almighty internal struggle for high places on the list. Only STV with its ability fairly to represent different strands within a party, according to the wishes of the electors, can hope to encourage harmony.

Is it not hypocritical of those MPs who cling to FPTP for their own elections to have any system but FPTP for everyone else's election?

The depth of public anger against individual MPs seen to have abused the parliamentary expenses system changed everything. For a time it stirred up open protest in a number of constituencies sufficient to catalyse a number of MPs into seeing electoral reform as a way of heading off broader protest. In its dying days, the Gordon Brown cabinet backed the idea of a referendum on electoral reform – though only with the feeble and often unproportional Alternative Vote (AV) as its preferred choice – but it only finally happened as an outcome of the subsequent Conservative/Liberal Democrat coalition, with the less than half-hearted support of the larger partner within that government, and without the full-hearted campaigning support of the opposition Labour party.

In politics it is always dangerous to opt for a small change when a significant reform is needed. The peers who clung on to power in 1909 and 1910 in the face of public opinion and democratic logic brought a more formidable constitutional change on themselves, not least because the prime minister, Asquith, knew that, if push came to shove, the king, supported by public opinion, would create enough new peers to force reform through.

Occasionally, in their anxiety to disparage proportional representation generally, leaders of Conservative and Labour parties over the years have given the game away. When he was prime minister, John Major stated that the Liberal Democrats favoured PR because it would put them permanently into government. Roy Hattersley, erstwhile Labour deputy leader and now a convert, used to oppose PR for Westminster because it would deny Labour the chance ever again to govern in its own right. It is an interesting admission that both parties believed their electoral appeal to be so weak that they accept for the foreseeable future that they could not conceive of attracting more than 50 per cent of the popular vote. To admit to such a lack of support and yet still claim the right to govern alone betrays a considerable arrogance and a curious conception of the concept of democracy.

The Liberal Democrats are regularly accused of wanting PR because it would benefit them as a party. Leaving aside the impossibility of ever being able objectively to determine motives, it may or may not be a reason, but the sources of the accusations are instructive. They come from both the Labour and Conservative parties who just happen to be the beneficiaries, in varying degrees at different elections, of the present system. They too can well be accused of having selfish motives for their objection to change. Accusations of self interest neatly balance each other out. They really ought to be set aside in favour of serious consideration of the relevant arguments.

The second major stumbling block has been the lack of consensus on the system to put in place of FPTP. From time to time the panacea of a referendum has been proposed as a way of avoiding the issue. If the question posed was simply one of a vague principle – 'Do you favour a change from the present voting system to one based on proportional representation?' – it would not resolve the issue. It begs the question of what kind of PR is in mind: representation of parties as parties, ie a list system, a preferential system of voting for candidates, or a hybrid mix of list and constituency. This major omission has bedevilled the referendum proposal for many reformers. Enough shrewd electors would make it clear that clear alternatives need to be on offer before they are prepared to cast their votes, otherwise, as we saw in May 2011, it undermines any referendum. Change at any price is not a rallying cry with much immediate resonance. In hindsight would the public have been happy at the time to have had the chance to vote to abandon the rating system without knowing in advance it would be replaced with the poll tax, or, indeed, with the council tax?

When Labour came into office in 1997 the then home secretary, Jack Straw, confirmed that there was to be an independent commission to recommend a proportional alternative to be put to the electorate at a referendum. The pre-election agreement between Labour and the Liberal Democrats[17] envisaged a referendum in time for its decision to be enacted before the following general election. The independent commission under Lord (Roy) Jenkins was duly appointed in December 1997 by the government and reported in September 1998, but two further general elections came and went without a sign of the promised referendum.

A campaign for a referendum on the voting system to take place on polling day alongside the general election vote gathered considerable momentum in the light of the exposure of the parliamentary expenses scandal as a number of ministers and leading MPs rightly saw electoral reform as one means of potentially giving the electorate more influence over the choice of its members of parliament. That campaign's aim was to put a specific alternative system up against FPTP at the proposed referendum. Given the different broad types of PR – list, mixed and preferential – it could well be argued that a multi-option referendum should be the target, but, if only one system was to be on the ballot paper in contention with FPTP, it was crucial that that system was the best option available – and certainly that was not AV, as eventually happened. The dissatisfaction with the mechanics of the 2010 referendum process and its failure to concentrate on the issues, as opposed to personal and party diversions, calls into question the efficacy of using referendums. The June 2016 referendum on the UK's membership of the European Union saw the same tactics, but even more marked. I would argue that the whole referendum process is flawed and all too susceptible to manipulation.

17 *Partnership for Britain's Future*, signed by Robin Cook and Robert Maclennan, January 1997.

SINGLE-MEMBER OR
MULTI-MEMBER?

O NE OF THE MOST PERVASIVE fallacies required to justify the present voting system is the almost mystical powers accorded to the single-member constituency. However, the attributes of the professed indispensability of the link between an individual MP and his or her constituency disintegrate in the face of thorough analysis. Quite apart from the way it blights other electoral reform, it also inhibits the wider choice of candidate.

Given the passion with which MPs defend the concept of the single-member constituency one might imagine that it has been written in stone since, say, the advent of the Reform Act of 1832. Far from it; in fact, in the 19th century there were a number of two-member and, later, three-member constituencies which, perforce, had representatives from different parties. Perhaps the best historical example of the benefits of the double-member constituency is that of Northampton where the great Liberal Radical and atheist, Charles Bradlaugh,[1] had been badly defeated when standing on his own as a plain Radical candidate. His supporters approached the Northampton Liberal party and offered to support any Liberal candidate provided that the Liberals would also back Bradlaugh. Thus, in partnership with Henry Labouchère, Bradlaugh was elected to parliament in 1880 and commenced his struggle to affirm rather than take the religious

---

1   See entry on Bradlaugh by Edward Royle in *Oxford Dictionary of National Biography*, 2011.

oath. Time after time the establishment's antagonism to Bradlaugh's atheism denied him the right to sit in parliament and caused him to contest Northampton successfully five times in five years before a new Speaker ruled him eligible.

One does not have to go back so far to find another example. Double-member constituencies continued in Britain until 1950 and the late Barbara Castle put it on record that she was convinced that, as a young radical woman, she would not have been selected for Blackburn in 1945 had it not been a two-member seat in which a 'safe' male candidate could also stand.[2]

This problem is further compounded by the trend to a monopoly of one-party representation in whole swathes of the country. Thus any argument for the accountability of an MP to a constituency is in practice confined to a small number of marginal seats. In far too many seats the MP can virtually ignore individual representations and still get re-elected at each election. In reality British society is nowhere near as politically divided as FPTP makes it appear. For instance, in 1931 – the most polarised general election in modern times – the National Government candidates secured 67 per cent of the vote and 90 per cent of MPs, whereas Labour got 31 per cent of the vote and only 9 per cent of MPs. Despite the size of the minority vote in a number of regions of Britain, it is not sufficient to secure individual seats. At the 2005 election, for instance, in my county of West Yorkshire, there was just one Conservative and one Liberal Democrat MP elected out of 23 despite those two parties between them securing 46 per cent of the vote. The results in 2010 were more spread but still well astray from any fair representation, with seven Conservative and two Liberal Democrat MPs out of the 23, despite having, jointly, 53 per cent of the vote. At the 2015 general election Labour still held on to 15 seats in West Yorkshire despite its vote dropping to 42 per cent. If members of a party sincerely believe that, in addition to the

2   Barbara Castle, *Fighting all the way*, Macmillan, 1993, p122 and Anne Perkins, *Red Queen*, Macmillan, 2003, p78.

advantages of their party's policies being influential in government, their MPs can best represent individuals and groups, why do they support an electoral system that ensures that whole areas of the country regularly minimise the benefits of that representation?

THE BROAD CHURCH

The single-member constituency in effect requires a party list of one. However strong the different tendencies within the local party, only the candidate of the dominant group will be chosen. To maximise their electoral chances under FPTP, parties have to produce large broad church organisations which are legitimate coalitions of varying strands and tendencies, even though it is manifestly impossible for the range of party opinions and styles to be represented through a single candidate in a single constituency. That, however, is exactly what the party has to pretend it is doing. The leaders of a party have publicly to urge the voters to support all its candidates across the country even though privately they are invariably wholly out of sympathy with a number of them. As prime minister from 1992, John Major famously talked about hearing 'the white coats flapping' in relation to a number of diehard anti-Europeans who undermined his government but who, of course, remained on the Conservative list of candidates, still led by John Major, at the next election in 1997.

Perhaps the pretence of the integrity of the single-member constituency was most vividly demonstrated throughout the more than 30 years that prime ministers Margaret Thatcher and Edward Heath represented their two London constituencies as Conservative MPs. How should a loyal Conservative have voted in Old Bexley and Sidcup if he or she was passionately in favour of Mrs Thatcher's view of British sovereignty? Conversely, what should a Tory loyalist in Finchley have done who supported Edward Heath's brand of European federalism? The internal party coalition required by FPTP is an insult to the intelligence of the voter. Political reality requires an acceptance of the legitimacy of the different strands within a party – as well as, for instance, of gender or race – and of the advantages of presenting a balanced team of candidates for the elector to put in order of his or her preference.

THE ALL-PURPOSE MEMBER

Given the firm convention that one MP does not interfere in another's constituency, the case for the single-member constituency requires the belief that the member thus elected is henceforth able to deal with every constituency matter that arises, whether it is an individual elector's problem or a local controversy. Of course, most MPs strive valiantly to achieve this, some more successfully than others, but, quite apart from the huge logistical problems involved, human nature itself undermines the principle.

For instance, I was approached by an Asian family desperate for help to prevent their young son being deported. As I came to the end of taking notes on the case, I discovered that they were not my constituents. Their own Conservative MP was unsympathetic to the case and had declined to make further representations. It would have been harsh and insensitive to have refused them the help that their case deserved but which the theory of the all-embracing single-member denies. I had to circumvent the convention by getting a Liberal peer to make the necessary representations.

The nonsense of the assumed constraint of the MP to deal only with his or her constituents was demonstrated recently when I took up an issue with the Conservative MP for Pudsey that manifestly concerned the entire city of Leeds. Eventually, I was informed on his behalf that he would not act on my representations because I was not his constituent! I pointed out that the issue involved was a whole city matter whereupon I was blithely told that it was not a priority because it had been raised by a non-constituent. Such is the deleterious effect of the single-member seat.[3]

3   See my letter 'Can there not be united action to save visitors' centre?' *Yorkshire Post*, 3 January 2015.

The same conflict arises on local issues of principle. Would a left-Labour MP be inclined to respond supportively to the local Chamber of Commerce's representations in favour of the privatisation of municipal services? Or would a Liberal Democrat MP be amenable to a request for help with a planning application to extend a chemical works near a residential area? And why should an elector be forced to approach an MP who is on the record as being – quite legitimately – opposed to a particular matter on which the elector wishes to seek help? Obviously some issues are more questions of principle than others, but I always felt sorry for constituents who had no choice but to approach me, say, for help in getting a son or daughter into a private school when my views on education were well known. Of course, I provided the information on the ways and means of obtaining assistance but it is not the same as being enthusiastic. None of these examples is particularly unusual and MPs of all parties would no doubt do their best within the confines of their consciences. But why should they be forced into a potentially uncomfortable compromise in order to defend an unnecessary electoral convention? A choice of local MPs would potentially give voters a better service.

Most MPs do faithfully attempt to cope with constituents' letters, emails, telephone calls and through their attendance at constituency surgeries, although I suspect that much of the rhetoric about casework paints a picture more glamorous than the reality. As it happens, I enjoyed being written about as being a good constituency MP, but I was very much aware that a great deal of the work that helped to build that reputation was carried out by my staff. They often got on with cases without referring to me and I was occasionally thanked by constituents in relation to help of which I was wholly unaware! I suspect also that, like me, every MP who marks the electoral register with all those she or he has been in direct contact with will be disappointed to find how few they are in reality. The impression one acquires of being personally in touch with thousands of electors is, alas, a great illusion.

Unlike many MPs, I had a compact inner city constituency and lived in the centre of it. Even so I found it difficult to keep track of events 'on the patch.' At first I found this frustrating but soon realised that it was a sign of healthy communities that much more was happening than I could keep abreast of, but the subtle pressure on the MP to have a finger in every pie still hovered. What little empirical evidence there is suggests that MPs have grossly inflated ideas about their impact in the constituency.[4] It is the desire to defend the single-member constituency concept that produces this need to pretend to have intimate knowledge of every nook and cranny, rather than vice versa.

The slow assassination of local democracy by successive governments since 1948 and the long diminution of municipal government have contributed substantially to the high level of MPs' local casework. I am probably now in a minority in believing that this is bad for MPs and detrimental to parliament's fundamental roles of holding the executive to account and of investigating and reporting on current issues, but I believe that it needs to be stated and that MPs should resist being pressured into being 'super councillors'. In urban areas, particularly where housing problems are widespread, over half the MP's casework may well fall more appropriately into the realm of local councillors' responsibilities. If the concern is that councillors are neither adequately representative nor clearly accountable the obvious answer is to use STV for local elections, as has already been done in Scotland, and then to restore powers to the municipalities. In its turn this would enable MPs to concentrate more on national and international concerns to the benefit of democracy in general in these difficult days.

I also suspect that more MPs than dare to admit it agree with the late Labour MP Tony Banks' comments in 2004, when announcing his retirement from parliament:

---

4   See, for instance, *Annual Audit of Political Engagement*, Hansard Society.

It's twenty-two years of the same cases, but just the faces and the people changing. I found it intellectually numbing, tedious in the extreme. It might sound a little disparaging to say this about people's lives and their problems and we did deal with them... but I got no satisfaction from this at all. I really didn't. And all you were was a sort of high-powered social worker and perhaps not even a good one. I won't miss that.[5]

The politicians may choose to ignore the problem, but the electors understand it well. An ERS/MORI opinion poll showed that 61 per cent of voters whose MP was of a different political persuasion from themselves favoured multi-member constituencies.[6] One suspects that a substantial number of individual casework problems are not taken to the MP at all because the MP concerned is thought – rightly or wrongly – to be unsympathetic. This suggests that a different and much more sympathetic system of relaying voter concerns to MPs singly, and to parliament generally, is needed. The single-member system is itself a significant barrier to a representative democracy appropriate to the 21st century.

ARTIFICIAL BOUNDARIES

Of course, the allegedly unique advantages of the single-member constituency require a belief that the electors are aware of which constituency they reside in. Alas, their innocent ignorance of constituency boundaries must all too often be a grave disappointment to the faithful MP. I had a number of visitors to my surgeries who assured me with touching earnestness that they had always voted for me. Unfortunately, knowing their addresses, I was aware that they had never lived within my patch! Even leaving aside the regular revision of constituency boundaries, which in itself illustrates the

5   Interview with Robin Oakley, BBC Radio 4, 26 November 2004.
6   Analysed by Shaun Bowler and David M Farrell, in *Representation* (McDougall Trust) vol 32, issue 120, 1994.

frailty of a democracy based on single-member constituencies which have continually to be redrawn, in a great many cases there is every excuse for such confusion. The coalition government's proposals for having fewer and larger constituencies and redrawing them every five years, based only on arithmetic and without reference to communities of interest, would fatally undermine any possibility of in-depth identification of an MP with local communities and of an MP 'nursing' a constituency. The Liberal Democrats eventually killed off this proposal but it might perhaps have been worth putting up with the disruption if it helped to expose the weakness of the single-member constituency. I assume that the Conservative government elected in 2015 will enact this change which it believes to be to its electoral advantage.

Constituency boundaries are often remarkably capricious. Again this can easily be illustrated from Leeds West, the constituency which I represented. In the one small neighbourhood of New Wortley, in Leeds 12, First Avenue and Second Avenue were in Leeds Central but Third Avenue was in Leeds West. In another, northern, part of the constituency in Leeds 6, the only place for a surgery was a library serving a clutch of adjacent terraced streets which were split between Leeds West and Leeds North West. In both cases people who turned up from the 'wrong' constituency were puzzled that I could not easily deal with their problems but had helped their neighbours. These anomalies are repeated in every urban area.

Only about one in ten constituencies can be said to be composed of clearly identifiable natural communities. The vast majority are artificial segments of a town or district or a forced amalgam of two or more district councils. Even in the constituencies that are arguably self-contained there are some covering district councils that are themselves somewhat artificial creations of local government reorganisation. This is even more the case with the advent of unitary authorities. The necessary obligation to have a rough equality of voters in over 600 single constituencies creates an insuperable problem and militates against the retention of communities of interest.

THE GOVERNMENT OPT-OUT

A further defect of the single-member constituency is that, because the government is regarded as being indivisible, members of it (and for very different reasons, the speaker and deputy speakers) do not table written or oral questions, do not sign motions and do not seek adjournment debates. Ministers do not participate in debates at all save as spokespersons for the government. All these restrictions deny their constituents key aspects of assistance and representation. It means that some 85 constituencies are partially disenfranchised. Even if it is alleged in defence of this damage to so many citizens, that ministers can exercise as much, if not more, influence behind the scenes on behalf of their constituents, this is at best unprovable and lacks the visibility and the public accountability that entries in Hansard ensure.

This drawback is acknowledged in that a minister may 'authorise' a constituent to go to another member. In this way I acquired an importunate constituent of Sir Keith Joseph, then MP for Leeds North-East, who had exhausted the remedies that the latter could employ whilst being a member of the government. The case required questions to be tabled to the attorney general which, of course, Sir Keith could not do. He therefore willingly accepted that his constituent could approach another MP.

So much for the single-member constituency and its protagonists' claims that its all-embracing and ubiquitous capacity can deal with each and every problem. It is highly unlikely that all MPs from a multi-member constituency would be in government at the same time so there would invariably be an MP able and willing to deal with a constituent's problem.

THE MATHEMATICAL IMPERATIVE

None of these arguments will necessarily inhibit an MP talking about 'my constituency' in almost proprietorial terms, even though they may not live in it and may have stood, or tried to stand, for other constituencies before securing the present seat, and may hold it only on a minority of votes. Even more cynical are those MPs who, having represented a marginal seat, have moved to a safer seat – taking the 'chicken run' as it is called – sometimes even before defending 'my constituency' at a general election.

Just in case listing the myths surrounding single-member seats is not enough in itself, it is important to recognise that the arguments against them for electoral reformers are, if anything, even more formidable. First and foremost, it is impossible to have both proportional representation and single-member constituencies. There is no way of carving up the United Kingdom into 600-plus separate seats that can produce anything other than a mathematical lottery. Even though the Boundary Commission is independent, its rules lay it open to political influence. I shamelessly made successful representations in 1983 in order to persuade the Commissioners to alter their initial proposals for Leeds West and thus produce a winnable seat. My representations were, of course, on objective grounds and the Commission's final plans were, of course, in the interests of preserving better communities of interest, but my political aim was achieved.

Anomalies can and do arise even where there are basically only two main parties, as in 1951 when the party that lost in terms of total votes cast won a majority of seats. But if, for instance, a third party, drawing its support evenly from left and right, was high in the polls, it would be perfectly possible for it to come second virtually everywhere, securing the highest total number of votes but not a single seat. This may sound fanciful, but it is not so distant from what happened in 1983 when, with only 2 per cent more votes nationally, Labour ended up with 269 seats and the Liberal-SDP Alliance had only 23 seats. In the 2015 general election, this disparity of votes and seats was particularly demonstrated by UKIP who polled almost four million votes but won only a single seat.

There is still sufficient class voting to ensure that Labour and Conservative parties are bound to elect substantial numbers of MPs but any relationship to total votes cast is purely coincidental, though the current rise of UKIP, the Green party and the SNP may, if only temporarily, disturb this assumption. Similar arguments apply to electoral systems which attempt to ameliorate the basic flaw in single-member seats, such as the Alternative Vote or the Second Ballot, sometimes favoured by the Labour party faithful in the fond belief that it might deceive reformers into thinking that they are favouring PR.

The argument *for* the multi-member constituency does not merely rest negatively on the many flaws in the case for the single-member seat. The positive arguments are clear.

Multi-member seats enable elected members to work as a team where and when they so wish, on local issues for instance, without the accusations of disloyalty or of threats of electoral disadvantage. They also enable electors to choose the most appropriate member or members to approach with an individual problem.

Flexibility as to numbers of representatives per constituency enables constituency boundaries to reflect more easily natural communities, rather than being carved up artificially to produce equal numbers of electors per single seat. Also the partial loss of representational rights that results from a single-seat MP joining the government is avoided.

The 1997 general election and, to some extent, subsequent elections, saw a significant increase in the number of women MPs elected but this was largely achieved by imposition from on high, often in the Labour party by all-women short lists. Such centralisation is unavoidable with FPTP. With STV in multi-member seats, the nomination of a balanced team of candidates by each party is encouraged, not least because to maximise the number of seats won the party needs to secure later preferences from electors who can be persuaded to move from their party allegiance in order to support, say, a woman or an ethnic minority candidate. For the parties to achieve a better balance under FPTP they have either to force out a sitting exemplar of the archetypal middle class, middle aged, middle-of-the-road, white male MP or wait impatiently for him to retire. Parties have to exercise influence but, under FPTP they are tempted to be over-dominant.

Multi-member seats are essential for achieving PR and for enabling virtually every elector to have at least one MP that he or she supports. Furthermore multi-member seat elections require preferential voting – in effect STV – if pre-election deals to deny voters a full choice are to be prevented. The current European Parliament election system is a perfect illustration; it has multi-member seats but the electors are denied any choice of candidate. The parties determine the list and electors have to vote for the party – and its list. The elector is unable to vote for an individual candidate. The essentially undemocratic nature of this system is demonstrated when a European MEP defects but can retain his or her seat despite being elected as a party list candidate. Many professional, trade union and other voluntary bodies today elect their management committees by STV because they have realised that dealing with a multi-member seat election by 'multiple X' voting is wholly unsatisfactory. With multiple X voting – that is placing an 'X' by every candidate for whom the elector wishes to vote up to the number to be elected – every vote for one candidate is mathematically a vote against all the others and, to maximise his or her chances of victory, an individual candidate needs to persuade the electors only to vote for himself or herself and not for any other candidate, whereas with STV, voters' wishes are followed in the order of priority in which they are indicated, without lower preferences detrimentally affecting earlier choices.

Despite all the arguments of principle, many present MPs remain publicly attached to the concept of the single-member seat. They have achieved election in such a seat and, over the years, they have come to feel that their relationship with their constituency is beneficial to their constituents and to their party. They may also worry that a different electoral system will disadvantage them personally. For a conscientious MP one great advantage of STV is that it ensures that the able, assiduous and well-established MP will poll well and has little to fear. Eventually, however, unless the terms of a referendum override a vote in the Houses of Parliament, it will be MPs elected for single-member seats, in an FPTP election, who are going to have to vote on electoral reform when it comes before the Commons. Far more important, though, alas, less immediate than present MPs supporting the system that elected them, in considering the benefits of one system over another, is whether the present system serves democracy and the political process effectively. And, if it doesn't, what is the alternative?

SYSTEMS

ONCE THE ARGUMENT FOR CHANGE has been engaged, the different voting systems need to be examined. To an extent, the case for reform has been weakened over the years by the failure of those wanting change to agree on what that change should be. The advocates of FPTP have always profited from the divisions amongst their opponents. Today's circumstances, with the 2015 election being the most unrepresentative ever, with alarming levels of public disrespect for MPs and a mistrust of political parties, need to be recognised when considering the best alternative to FPTP.

The dangerous misconception often demonstrated in simplistic discussions of voting systems is that there is somehow a continuous line of improvement from FPTP towards 'higher' versions of proportional representation. There isn't. Electoral systems have very different characteristics and effects and it is these that need to be considered.

There are three groups, or families, of voting systems:

- **plurality systems** which utilise single-member seats in which, to be elected, a candidate has only to secure the highest number of votes – whether or not that figure is an overall majority;
- **list systems** where parties are voted for rather than candidates;
- **preferential systems** in which candidates are ranked in order, rather than voted for with an 'X'.

Inevitably, numerous attempts are made to ameliorate the perceived defects of each system, as we shall now see.

THE ALTERNATIVE VOTE AND THE SECOND BALLOT

There are two ways by which the FPTP system is 'improved'. Under the Alternative Vote (AV) electors mark the candidates 1, 2, 3 ... in order of preference in a single-member constituency. This enables the redistribution of the votes of the candidate or candidates with the least support until one candidate has more than 50 per cent of the remaining votes. It thus attempts to produce a parliament that accords to voters' preferences, however, in reality, it almost invariably restricts voters to single candidates from, and chosen by, each party. What is more, in the attempt to demonstrate that the winning candidate has majority support, electors are forced, in order for their votes to be effective, to vote more or less reluctantly for a candidate from a different party from their first choice, rendering any argument that the overall result represents genuine party preferences highly questionable. An editorial in *The Observer* commented:

> AV ... doesn't allocate parliamentary seats in line with the parties' national share of the vote. A better system is the single transferable vote, where voters also give numerical preferences, but a number of seats are awarded per constituency. That way, MPs are still bound to represent a fixed locality, but the final make-up of Parliament is an accurate reflection of national opinion.[1]

In addition, research has shown that elections under the Alternative Vote can be even less representative than straight FPTP. The political implications of the Alternative Vote are interesting. In 1991 when tactical voting was all the rage nationally, rather than just being a deliberate and partially successful Liberal Democrat strategy, a Rowntree Trust/MORI poll[2] suggested that many voters favoured a 'centre' party as their second choice, rather than switching right across

---

1   *The Observer,* 26 July 2009.
2   See: https://www.ipsos-mori.com/researchpublications/
researcharchive/2746/State-of-the-Nation-Survey-1991.aspx

to the other main party. Under AV, the likelihood is that when a second choice, if exercised, had to go to another party, the Liberal Democrats would benefit significantly. Fairness to minority parties is one thing, but preferential treatment may well be thought to be going too far.

Politically, the fact that AV was comprehensively rejected in the referendum of May 2011 probably means that it is no longer a future possibility. Even though it is not possible for a No campaign again to focus so much of its case personally against Liberal Democrat party leader Nick Clegg, simply to repeat a referendum with the same question as before is not a realistic political option.

The whole process was deeply frustrating to most of those who have been committed to electoral reform for many years. Some who nevertheless campaigned for AV saw it as a poor substitute for STV. Apart from other defects, it would not even produce party proportionality. Some others were dismayed by much of the negative and personality-centred campaigning tactics, and felt that it called into question the viability of any referendum as a vehicle for change. It is worth noting that the seven other devolved, European and local government bodies in the UK, with different electoral systems, were all initiated without any recourse to referendums.

The Jenkins Commission,[3] chaired by Lord (Roy) Jenkins in 1998, came out in favour of a system which became known as the Alternative Vote Plus (AV+). This was, in effect, a wholly new variant of the 'added members' genre and this gave the Labour government a somewhat spurious excuse for delaying the promised referendum, ie that it had to take time to consider in great detail the implications of this novel system. AV+ is a hybrid system that, like other additional member systems, uses a second ballot to redress the disproportionate effects of the first, constituency, vote. Under AV+ there would be an Alternative Vote ballot for somewhat larger single-member constituencies than presently exist. At the same time, electors would

---

3 For a good summary and analysis, see House of Commons Library Research Paper, 98/112.

vote in a second ballot, for which the designated constituency would be a whole region, so that the preferred candidates would 'top up' a party's representation in a region where it did not have sufficient MPs in proportion to the results of the first ballot. This idea not only produces two different types of MP – one with a local constituency and one without – a flaw even more evident in additional member systems, as dealt with below. It also means that candidates who lost in the first ballot and were, in effect, rejected by the electors, would often be elected in the second.

There is a further significant and highly topical difficulty with AV+. The exposure of a number of MPs allegedly abusing their parliamentary allowances has led to demands from electors to be able to vote against a sitting member without having to vote against their party. Only STV actually permits this, but imagine the electors' anger when, if so great is the antipathy to a retiring MP that he or she is defeated in the Alternative Vote first ballot, he or she is then elected in the much wider regional constituency for the second ballot. It would hardly improve the electorate's respect for the parliamentary process.

The French use the Second Ballot as a variant of the Alternative Vote. At the national level it involves two separate rounds of voting a fortnight apart in constituencies where no single candidate secures over 50 per cent of the vote. All candidates polling below 12.5 per cent are automatically excluded from the second ballot, but, usually, negotiations between parties ensure that only one left and one right candidate contests the second round. The advent of the far right Front National has produced three second-round candidates in an increasing number of constituencies. The aim of the Second Ballot is to give electors another opportunity to choose an MP when the first ballot has been indecisive but it again forces electors to choose from a restricted list carved out by private deals between parties, and excludes candidates for whom they may well have preferred to vote in the light of the first ballot. Any claims that it can produce proportionality are as weak as for the Alternative Vote.

In UK parliamentary elections the politics of the Second Ballot would probably be different from those of the Alternative Vote. The considerable pressure to have only two candidates in the second round encourages left-right polarisation and, in France, it has been a significant factor in the break up of the once dominant Radical party, vestiges of which are now found in three different French political *rassemblements*, as well as amongst the independents in the French National Assembly. A centre party is faced with the dilemma of doing a deal with one side or the other – and probably splitting the party – or continuing with a third candidate wherever it polls more than 12.5 per cent, thus vitiating the whole point of the system. In France the second round often attracts a higher turnout than the first, whereas, in Britain, apart from a minority of committed politicians who are addicted to elections, the concept of two polling days a fortnight apart is unlikely to be thought feasible.

PARTY LISTS

All systems based on party lists require the parties to draw up lists of candidates to fill large multi-member constituencies. In Israel, the whole country is a single constituency in which a party wins a proportional number of seats if it polls over the threshold of 3.25 per cent of the votes cast. Thus a politician who falls out with party colleagues can all too easily form a new party and, if it can win around just 125,000 votes, that politician will remain a member of the Knesset, Israel's parliament. In contrast even with other regional systems, it is, however, an extremely proportional system for parties – but its detrimental effects on effective governance in Israel demonstrate that party proportionality is but one aspect of electoral reform. In fact, given the veto on government policy which the system provides to small religious parties, it is clear that Israel is a prime candidate for STV in which the threshold for getting elected would be significantly higher and would very likely give Israel a Knesset with far more political coherence and potentially greater effectiveness.

Even with regional lists and, consequently, higher thresholds for election than a system such as Israel's there are serious drawbacks. In particular, party lists give immense power to political parties. The party determines the order in which candidates secure election and the elector is unable to vote for an individual candidate – he or she in fact acquires members of parliament rather than electing them. The severance of the link between voter and representative destroys the direct accountability of an elected MP to his or her electorate. Unlike STV, constituencies are so huge as to be meaningless. Lists tend to encourage conformity to the party in order to secure an electable place on the list, and, in practice, this system has discriminated against women and ethnic minorities. By effectively transferring the real election to an internal party contest list, systems deny key choices to the electorate at large. The individual MP is virtually a party delegate whose main philosophic and policy activity is directed to the internal task of changing the party platform rather than winning electoral support. As a congenital party hack myself, I can see great advantages in increasing party control, but as a democrat I regard it as an anathema. Party hegemony is encouraged at the expense of pluralism – and this country desperately needs more pluralism and not less.

An MP or candidate who treasures even a modicum of independence and individuality could never support any list system, nor can I envisage the public being keen to swap the present voting for candidates representing parties for voting for parties who determe the list of candidates. Given the outcry over the parliamentary expenses scandal of 2009, electors would certainly be outraged if told that they could not demonstrate at the polls their opinion of an MP who had transgressed. Looking at the broader effects of lists, if the threshold for election is low, as in Israel, it encourages parties to split; if it is high it encourages entryism to manipulate the list which would provoke still more of the internal party strife which has debilitated British politics in recent years.

Allowing electors to vary the list as presented by the party improves things somewhat but evidence from countries where this is done suggests that most electors accept the party's candidate order and that the internal struggle for high places on the list is just as intense. Also, if electors are only allowed to choose between candidates of their preferred party, as opposed to across parties, it becomes an invitation for candidates to campaign personally against their own party colleagues rather than against other parties. Today, when the public is at its most cynical in regard to its view of political parties, is hardly the time to opt for any voting system that puts more power into party hands.

THE ADDITIONAL MEMBER SYSTEM

The Additional Member System (AMS) is used in Germany to achieve proportionality of party representation by the use of a second vote for a party list to compensate for the inevitable distortion of single-member constituencies. It is sometimes presented as being a good compromise between FPTP and full party lists whereas, in actual fact, it is arguably the worst of all worlds, combining as it does the faults of two systems whilst hardly diminishing each's inherent defects. Moreover, it fails the equal value test by electing two different categories of MP: those with constituency responsibilities and those without.

AMS cannot avoid the problem of selection procedures to determine the order of candidates on the list. Dr Dietrich Sperling MdB, the centre-left SPD's constitutional affairs frontbencher, explained the SPD's system:

> The conferences putting up the lists are normally following decisions of local organisations, demanding priority for their 'directly elected' (constituency) candidate. Exceptions are made for the top of the list (only).[4]

---

4   John Wheatley Centre conference, 23 February 1990.

The existence of the single-member seats does not inhibit the party organisations from doing battle over the list and does not prevent any of the internal problems associated with lists generally. In many cases those elected on the list were defeated in a constituency. As with the occasionally heard arguments that the best losers should have first claim on the list – as in effect in Jenkins' AV+ proposals – its democratic credentials are rather dubious. The democratic nonsense of the claims made for AMS by those keen to retain single-member constituencies was demonstrated by European parliament official Dr Philip Cole:

On the night of December 2nd 1990 there was an unusual air of excitement in Wuppertal, a dreary industrial city of over a third of a million in the Ruhr famous for having the highest railway bridge in Europe. Who would capture constituency 69 in the first all-German election for over half a century: Hans Dietrich Genscher (FDP), the outgoing Foreign Minister, Rudolf Dressler (SPD) or Peter Hintze (CDU)?

The excitement soon evaporated when it became clear that all three had been elected. The same pattern began to emerge all over the Federal Republic. Chancellor Kohl won a constituency seat (Ludwigshafen) for the first time ever but Reimann his defeated Socialist opponent was also returned to Parliament; in Berlin-Neukolln the SPD's president, Hans-Jochen Vogel, was elected despite winning only 31.8 per cent of the vote to the CDU candidate's 25.2 per cent; in Berlin-Hellersdorf two of Dr Gysi's (PDS) 'defeated' rivals also secured election to the Bundestag.

There is an unexpectedly surreal quality to elections to the Federal Republic and it is appropriate to examine why the German system is by no means as attractive as its advocates claim, since a broadly similar form of PR – the Additional Member System – has been proposed for Britain.[5]

5 Philip Cole, 'The German Bundestag election of December 2 1990' in *Representation* (McDougall Trust) vol 30, issue 110, 1991.

AMS requires huge single-member constituencies. In Germany they are almost three times the size of UK seats and, if half the House of Commons is to be elected from the list, they are bound on average to be twice the present size.

The more conscientious the MP the more they are likely to drive themselves into the ground trying to cope with vast increases in casework, particularly Labour MPs in seats with high levels of social and economic need. Given this significant flaw it was surprising that a version of AMS, called the Supplementary Vote, was favoured by Labour's Plant Commission, chaired by King's College Professor, later Lord, Raymond Plant in 1993.[6]

The real political killer, however, is the fact that conscientious MPs can be undermined politically by the intervention, perfectly legitimately, of an MP or MPs elected from the list and with no constituency responsibilities of their own. Have Labour MPs in particular considered the situation in which, at polling levels in recent elections, there would be many Liberal Democrat MPs elected from the list able to target any seat they felt vulnerable to being gained at the following general election and descending in droves without any threat to their own survival? AMS survives in Germany because, unlike in Britain, there is virtually no tradition of MPs having a close involvement in casework for individual constituents.

In Wales, with an AMS system, Labour members of the assembly, became so frustrated at the activities of Welsh Nationalist assembly members (elected from the lists) in certain target seats that they got the Labour government to put a bill through the UK parliament prohibiting a candidate from standing in both the constituency and list ballots.[7] When he introduced the ban, the then secretary of state for Wales, Peter Hain, said it was an abuse of the system to allow candidates to get elected on regional lists when they had lost First-Past-The-Post contests

---

6 See *The Plant Report, Third Report of Labour's Working Party on Electoral systems*, The Labour Party, 1993.

7 Clause 7 of the *Government of Wales Act 2006*.

in constituency elections. He thus identified a key defect in Additional Member electoral systems. Later, with the coalition government in place, much to the chagrin of this former Labour cabinet minister, by now Labour's shadow secretary of state for Wales, and the Welsh Labour party, the ban was lifted by the new government.[8]

A further curious anomaly of the Scottish and Welsh regional top-up systems is that fairly often they give extra seats to parties that are already over-represented nationally.

AMS is by far the optimum electoral system for benefiting the Liberal Democrats as a party. It gives them a proportionate number of MPs plus a marvellous organisational springboard for subsequent elections. The one extra refinement required to perfect the system for the Liberal Democrats' self-interest would be that proposed by the Jenkins Commission: to elect the constituency MPs by the Alternative Vote. This would give the Liberal Democrats more individual seats whilst still preserving their capacity, legitimately under this sytem, to use list MPs to their best advantage.

Political parties are essential components of our democratic process. At their best they provide a vehicle for topical political debate around a philosophical basis and can bring together those broadly of a like mind to campaign for their views to be supported by the electorate in order to bring them into legislation. They can, as such, provide the voter with a choice between clear options, with alternative ideological views of the way society should be organised. At worst they provoke a slanging match, all too often on a negative basis, which is increasingly seen by the electorate as unedifying and unattractive. More and more the parties, at both national and local levels attempt, where they are in a majority, to impose their narrow party rule further and further down the administrative chain – however precarious their control is arithmetically. These hegemonic tendencies have been matched by largely vain attempts to mitigate their effects by rules on twin tracking, on opposition rights, standards boards and client charters.

8   Clause 2 of the *Wales Act 2014*.

All these latter initiatives are only palliatives and weak attempts to find substitutes for a better democracy.[9]

Pluralism and diversity are not going to emerge from attempts to impose civilised rules of behaviour on reluctant party hierarchies as opposed to the adoption of an electoral system that rewards it. Electoral systems influence greatly the style and power of parties and this is not the moment to enhance the power and influence of the central party organisations by introducing further list systems – whether with complete lists or the half lists of AMS. Lists also make parties lazy and what is desperately needed is a means of diminishing the influence of the party over its selection and imposition of candidates whilst encouraging it to enter into political debate. More intellectual rigour is needed in the hope of thus attracting new candidates and of persuading electors to support it out of identification with its ideals and policies.

THE SINGLE TRANSFERABLE VOTE

I reiterate that no electoral system is perfect. However, whereas the present FPTP system, other single-member constituency systems and party lists are all incapable of satisfying one or more of the key democratic objectives of electoral systems (see page 15), the Single Transferable Vote best meets the key criteria as a whole. Other systems may satisfy one or other point better but then fail to meet others at all adequately. STV can also be used at each level of government, thus providing a valuable consistency. It was not surprising that in a survey of electoral systems in *The Guardian*,[10] STV was the only one to score five stars!

STV requires multi-member constituencies in which electors vote by marking the candidates 1, 2, 3 ... in order of preference, instead of using 'X' – the mark of illiteracy. Electors may vote for candidates

---

9   For a longer discussion of this issue see my book *Diversity in Danger*, Beecroft Publications, 1989.

10   Julian Glover, 'Electoral systems: alternative voting, and other alternatives', *The Guardian*, 27 May 2009.

within parties and across parties, and for independents. To be elected a candidate must obtain a quota of votes. This is simply the minimum number of votes needed to ensure election if all the votes cast are divided as equally as is possible across all the candidates. The quota is, therefore, the total number of votes cast divided by one more than the number of vacancies, plus one vote. No more than the required number of candidates to fill the seats available can mathematically reach this quota. For example, to guarantee election in a single-member seat a candidate has to get 50 per cent plus one of the votes cast. In a two-member seat it is therefore 33 per cent plus one vote, in a three-member seat it is 25 per cent plus one vote and so on.

STV is so called because it is based on the principle that the elector has a single first choice of representative but if that preferred candidate either has so many votes that the individual's vote is not needed, or has the least chance of being elected, then his or her vote is transferred pro rata to a second or subsequent choice. Thus in an STV election almost every vote counts towards the election of a candidate. Hardly any votes are wasted.

The mathematical formula to implement the principle may initially seem complex but quickly becomes clear through usage and operates under rules which, for instance, have been accepted over decades in both the Republic of Ireland and Northern Ireland. In 2007, STV was also introduced for Scottish local government elections, where voters had far less trouble coping with voting by preference than they did in dealing with the additional member system used for electing the Scottish Parliament at the same time. The second STV election for Scottish local authorities in 2012 appeared to be accepted by the electorate and the parties as normal. The follow-up report for the Electoral Commission stated: 'It is clear that the vast majority of electors are able to cope with the demands of the system.'[11] The assurance for the voter is that the competing parties and candidates

11 Hugh Bochel, David Denver and Martin Stevens, *Report on Scottish Local Elections 2012*, Universities of Lincoln and Lancaster, July 2012.

accept the validity of the formula and monitor the count. A modicum of complexity would seem a small price to pay in order to get the best system. A manual STV count may take a little more time than a count under FPTP but there are computer programs that cope securely and transparently with the count.

At the time of the 2009 local and European elections Fintan O'Toole, the assistant editor of the *Irish Times*, compared the effect of his vote in Ireland under STV with voting under FPTP in Britain.[12] It would be well worth quoting the whole article but the extracts below will have to suffice. He wrote that:

> According to David Blunkett... I will leave the polling booth feeling 'disempowered'. Actually, if thirty years of using a proportional representation system of voting is anything to go by, I'll be feeling rather powerful.

He went on to compare his choices with the problem in Britain of either voting tactically or wasting one's vote in an FPTP election:

> I can vote for someone who represents my minority views, knowing that if she or he does not get elected, my vote will be transferred to my second choice, and so on down the line.

O'Toole goes on to make the point that:

> What politicians like [David] Blunkett, who say they are in favour of reform, should be arguing about is not whether to have a PR system, but which PR system to have. He is right to be wary of list systems that produce 'placemen with no constituency accountability'.

He continues with the point that the Irish system of multi-seat constituencies has 'some drawbacks', but concludes with a powerful message to entrenched and complacent British views that change would also:

---

12 *The Observer*, 31 May 2009.

... [require] the humility to stop patronising voters. The real opposition to PR lies in the deep-seated belief that voters shouldn't be given too many choices because they'd only misuse them. Voters have the right to make things more complicated than the political class would want. It's called democracy.

Fintan O'Toole is right: it is typical of the British approach to politics that there are so many movers and shakers who think it is possible to solve complex problems with simple solutions. This attitude applied to the financial regulation of banking was one key cause of the collapse of that industry. Politicians are at last discovering that there are no pat answers to the global problem of climate change. Why should the politicians believe that there is also a facile answer to the deep-seated problems of our democratic processes? Why prefer electoral systems that cannot deal with the issue rather than adopting the one that has the best possibility of doing so? STV certainly requires somewhat more explanation, but it is clear from its long use in the Republic of Ireland, Northern Ireland and, more recently, its introduction in Scotland that it poses no serious difficulty to the electors.

Because constituencies are multi-member the number of seats in each one can vary, depending on natural boundaries, so that the artificiality of carving segments out of a city, or tacking odd bits of countryside onto a town to make up the voter numbers, can be avoided. In Ireland constituencies elect three, four or five members. A similar provision of minimum and maximum seats per constituency could be made for the United Kingdom – preferably with a slightly higher maximum to reflect the larger population concentrations in Britain.

All the major parties have expressed concern at the desperately low representation of women and of ethnic minorities in parliament. With STV and multi-member constituencies, parties would have a powerful incentive to present a balanced team of candidates in order to maximise the number of higher preferences that would go to their sponsored candidates. There may well be some electors who, quite legitimately, will give their high preferences all to women candidates across the parties and a party which does not seek to attract such sectional voters will lose out. I do not believe that enough single-member constituencies will ever willingly depart significantly from adopting the traditional 'safe' candidate, thus denying the electors the chance to redress the present gender and ethnic parliamentary imbalances. Labour's recourse to forcing all-women shortlists on to constituencies often leaves a very sour taste in the constituency association.[13]

An argument used against multi-member constituencies has been the inherent need to have rural constituencies covering large areas. It is a genuine argument and, if having smaller constituencies in, say, the Scottish highlands, islands and borders, as compared with large constituencies in Glasgow and Edinburgh, is considered to favour the Liberal Democrats electorally, then it may still be necessary to have a minimum of three or four-member seats even in such areas. The previous single-member European Parliament constituencies, before Scotland was a single-list system constituency, were of comparable size without apparently insuperable logistical difficulties.

A crucial advantage of STV is that the constituency link is retained, albeit with several MPs in a larger constituency. The accountability of MPs to their constituents is actually increased in that, unlike British single-member constituencies, no individual MP has a safe seat. The quid pro quo for this diminution of security of tenure in certain seats is that the multi-member constituency and STV between them provide a broader basis for all MPs to win on merit, however brave or even foolhardy they may be in promoting unpopular views. Even deselection as such by the party is not necessarily electorally fatal. Back in 1972, in Donegal, in the Republic of Ireland, long-serving

---

13 See, for instance, the long row in 2014 in the Cynon Valley constituency: http://www.bbc.co.uk/news/uk-wales-politics-28156857. Also, in the Blaenau Gwent constituency, Peter Law resigned from the Labour party over the imposition of an all woman shortlist and then fought and won the seat as an independent in 2005.

member of parliament and minister Neil Blaney was dropped by his party, Fianna Fail, after dubious arms dealings, but he was re-elected as an independent TD at the subsequent election and each time until his death in 1993. In effect, the parties put forward their preferred lists of nominees at each election but, under STV, each elector can determine his or her own list of preferred candidates.

If the argument is that identity with an electoral area assists accountability then STV certainly helps by giving electors a natural link with a city or a county rather than with a geographic segment drawn artificially to try and maintain equality of numbers in single-member constituencies. Electors may well prefer to have real influence over the MPs representing the whole city or county rather than struggle to hold the one MP for their sector accountable. Multi-member seats are, of course, the norm for local government where the concept of working as a team for a local ward is often seen to be advantageous. In Scottish local government, following the introduction of STV, there is already evidence that ward councillors see the advantage – and the electoral imperative – of co-operation.[14] If MPs, representing a city or a county, develop subject or local interests within their constituency, in addition to individual constituents' concerns, that is surely a bonus for the electors.

Some of the criticisms of STV voiced by the Jenkins Commission in 1998 have since been addressed by the successful introduction of the system for Scottish local government. No longer would STV 'be too big a leap from that to which we have become used.'[15] Even the Jenkins argument that 'it would be a leap in a confusingly different direction from other electoral changes which are currently being made in Britain,'[16] is undermined by the increasingly articulated criticisms

---

14 See Electoral Reform Society publications on Scotland: http://www.electoral-reform.org.uk/publications/
15 'The Single Transferable Vote' in The Report of the Independent Commission on the Voting System, (Chair Lord Jenkins) October 1998, ch 6.
16 Jenkins Commission, op cit.

of additional-member systems in Scotland and Wales. It is significant that in both countries, commissions dealing with the subject – Richard in Wales[17] and Arbuthnott in Scotland[18] – have advocated either a change to STV for the elections to the assembly or consideration of it for those to the parliament respectively.

To some extent the Jenkins Commission made the error of under-estimating the electorate. My experience around the world, in new and emerging democracies, is that even apparently unsophisticated electorates are well able to cope with seemingly complex electoral arrangements, and I do not see why the British electorate should be thought incapable or even unwilling to cope with indicating its candidate preferences on a ballot paper. Jenkins does acknowledge its impression that 'STV in Ireland is perhaps more popular with the public than with the politicians,' but then, rather curiously, says that, 'if this be so it is difficult to know whether to score the point in the favourable or the adverse list.' It is rather more concrete than an impression, given that on two occasions in referenda the Irish electorate has rejected the politicians' attempts to get rid of STV.[19] And, even with my long party history and strong belief in the crucial importance of political parties, I would count public popularity as a plus.

Jenkins has another rather disdainful criticism of STV: 'Some people want to be able to choose between candidates of the same party, but many are interested only in voting for parties, and would not appreciate being forced into choosing between candidates of the same party about each of whom they know little.' This may indeed be true, but to a greater or lesser extent, it is a product of FPTP (and of the European Parliament elections in which an elector is actually

17 *Report of the Richard Commission*, Spring 2004, pp235-236.
18 *Putting Citizens First: Boundaries, Voting and Representation in Scotland*, (Chairman James Arbuthnott), January 2006, p53.
19 In 1959 and 1968 the Irish Government tried to get rid of the single transferable vote but on each occasion the electorate voted to retain it. For further information see Michael Gallagher and Paul Simpson (eds), *The Politics of Electoral Systems*, Oxford University Press, 2005.

forced to vote for a party and not a candidate) in which the party presents a 'take it or leave it' choice. It may well be that being offered a wider choice will help to rekindle the voters' interest in politics and in parties. In any case, if a voter is only interested in voting for the party, then he or she simply needs to follow the advice that will be given by the party as to its preferred party candidate choices, and need go no further down the list. There is no question of being forced into anything. It is entirely the voter's choice.

The present party system in Britain has come under increasing criticism in recent years – even from party members themselves. The declining membership of all mainstream parties; the tensions between the centre and the constituency associations; the ability of party leaders to dominate their parties, often through use of the media; the philosophic divisions or the lowest common denominators brought about by the need for a broad church; the emphasis on negative or tactical voting; and the basic superficiality and short-term emphasis of political debate, have all been the subject of criticism. It is not as if the public is any less political than it once was: the membership of ecological organisations and the massive public demonstrations on issues, such as those against the Iraq invasion and at the G20 summit, are clear evidence of that. It is just the particular disillusion with political parties that characterises today's politics. The spike in Labour party membership with Jeremy Corbyn's leadership candidature has some similarities with this 'anti politics' trend.

The 2009 parliamentary expenses scandal added to this view. As was noted earlier, even the main parties' treatment of this scandal showed the dangers of the FPTP system with the Conservative leader apparently able to force MPs to stand down at the 2010 election, and with a Labour party 'Star Chamber' able to play the same arbitrary role. Only STV permits an elector to continue to vote for his or her party whilst being able to vote against an individual candidate. If the parties wish to reinvent themselves as political organisations worthy of support, they really ought to take note of this.

Hitherto the prospect of electoral reform having an important role in influencing party structures and styles has seemed to alarm the politicians. Far simpler and safer to hang on to what they know rather than have to contemplate significant changes. How far down does the public support for the current structures have to go before the politicians are prepared to swallow hard and to grasp the risks? Before long it will be the abyss rather than the crystal ball. Any change in the electoral system will affect the nature of politics; the issue is whether the possibility of improvement is worth the risks involved. At least the 2009 expenses revelations brought a number of untarnished senior MPs out of the woodwork, including Alan Johnson, John Denham, James Purnell and Roy Hattersley who openly supported a change to proportional systems, and not just to AV.

Under STV, with voters able to express as many preferences as they wish, it is impossible to vote negatively. Parties will need to respond to this by developing policies and campaigning styles to attract a wider cross-section of support rather than being able to rely on the support of electors voting against one party or another. The likelihood is, given the strong traditions of tightly structured parties in Britain, that the present broad church will continue, though individual candidates or groups of candidates will be in a stronger position to promote their particular stance on issues. The party leadership will not have as much direct control of its troops as hitherto but it will no doubt put up with this in order to keep the party together. It is arguable, of course, given the remarkable levels of rebellion by Labour and Conservative MPs against their party whips in recent years,[20] that this trend is already well underway. If this is indeed the case, it will make for a smoother transition to the style of party politics that would arrive with STV.

Only if there is persistent opposition to the main thrust of the party will there be the tendency to split and fight separately or as an associated group – and it is arguable that in such circumstances either would be the appropriate and legitimate course of action. To cope with STV elections

20 See http://revolts.co.uk/ for details.

a party will have to deepen its own internal debating and consultation processes in order to develop more commitment to its basic philosophy, rather than relying simply on the discipline of the election 'coupon.' A party's central bureaucracy may well prefer a list system – including AMS – which strengthens its control, but the party as a whole would surely prefer the gains to party democracy which STV would bring. It would be likely to encourage the revival of party politics generally and the recruitment of more candidates at all levels.

Concern has been expressed that under STV there will be electoral competition between candidates of the same party and indeed there might be. Given the strength of the British party system, in most cases party solidarity and loyalty would inhibit individualistic campaigning, but even were it to happen it must be regarded as a trade off against the present ability of a party simply to exclude from the ticket a recalcitrant candidate, whether rightly or wrongly. The party endorsement would still count for a great deal, even if it would not have quite the malevolent force that it can have under FPTP. The Irish academic Michael Gallagher argued that there is no reduction in the cohesion of parties in the Irish Republic, elected by STV, stating that in the Dàil, 'it is very rare for party representatives to break ranks from the party line on any issue.'[21]

The fear that STV will result in extra casework for MPs for their electoral survival, is unlikely to be justified, particularly given the level that MPs already do under FPTP. As argued earlier, the answer to the inordinately high levels of MPs' casework load is to enhance local government and for local councillors to do the casework on subjects that clearly belong at the local level. Even in Ireland where it is often alleged that STV produces high levels of casework – and where there are few powers at the local government level – the experience is that it is not a particularly significant problem and that it is largely limited to those constituencies in which there is competition for a single extra

21 Michael Gallagher and Paul Simpson (ed), *The Politics of Electoral Systems*, Oxford University Press, 2005.

party seat. Moreover, Michael Gallagher has demonstrated[22] that there is no evidence that levels of casework are significantly different when there is only a single candidate from a party.

Of course, there is intra-party competition in every electoral system. With FPTP, it is internalised within the selection and re-selection process; with party lists it becomes a permanent internal competition for a high place on the list. Experience is that that competition can be extremely tough, and, of course, it puts a high premium on conformity rather than independence of mind. The question, as ever, is whether the package of benefits that flow from STV enhances the democratic process more effectively than the possible alternatives.

In any case, to maximise its total support in a multi-member constituency, a party is likely to nominate a balanced team of candidates. It is worth bearing in mind that under STV all existing MPs can stand for election and, with their experience and public exposure, may well have an advantage in being better known than their newer party colleagues. Current party structures and practices are in many cases unhealthy and have prevented the parties from coming to terms with modern political challenges. These party structures are often the consequence of the exigences of the FPTP system. They may have delivered a particular type of MP and enabled the party to enforce its discipline under threat of deselection, but they also led to a massive decline in party membership and to a majority of candidates having a much narrower experience of life generally.

Replacing FPTP with STV will no doubt have an effect on party style but it will give parties the impetus to make changes for the better rather than remain locked in methods and tactics that appear to have less and less resonance with the public.

Because STV gives much more influence to the individual voter to determine a preferred order of preference within and across parties,

22 Michael Gallagher, 'Does Ireland need a new electoral system?' in *Irish Political Studies*, vol 2, issue 1, 1987.

strict party proportionality is more difficult to determine statistically. Those voters who wish to vote for the party ticket and nothing else are perfectly entitled to do so – and STV will guarantee to them that in, say, a five member seat, every 17 per cent or so of such votes will elect an MP of that party. However, because expressing a later preference cannot possibly affect an earlier one, voters under STV usually appreciate the importance of also being able to influence which member or members of other parties than their own should be elected and therefore do carry on expressing their preferences.

Even the Conservative Research Department, in a 1991 paper, basically critical of proportional representation, was forced to concede that:

> STV produces a high level of proportionality while retaining some of the elements of a constituency-based system. Furthermore, voters are able to choose between different candidates from the same party and can therefore try to secure the representation of a wider range of opinion – or alternatively endeavour to strengthen the representation of their favoured wing of the party.[23]

In other words it does, in a wider and more formal way, what David Cameron attempted to do in his support for open primaries to select Conservative prospective candidates – involve the wider public in choosing from the party's shortlist. Reducing the party membership's role in choosing the party's nominees, as proposed by Cameron, would be yet another disincentive to joining a party, whereas STV opens up the public's choice from amongst party nominees, and others.

STV is much more sophisticated than some commentators would like and there is often a rather simplistic tendency to equate first preference votes for candidates with exclusive electoral support for that candidate's party. For perfectly legitimate reasons,

23 *Proportional Representation,* Politics Today, Pamphlet No.12, Conservative Research Department paper, September 1991.

voters may well give their first preference to a candidate of another party – or to an independent – rather than to a candidate of their favoured party, if any. They may wish, for instance, to place a female candidate first if their own party has put forward an all male list. Thus any assessment of narrow party proportionality under STV needs to be made with some caution. The key point about STV is that it reflects the individual's voting intentions proportionally on the widest possible range of considerations far better than any other system – and certainly on a wider basis than simply party considerations. Every vote has equal value and the low number of wasted votes, ie. those which fail to elect any candidate of the voter's choice, is its greatest asset, and will reward the best in party politics, just as it will penalise the worst.

Electors are well able to cope with an STV ballot paper. A useful example is that of the first Northern Ireland Assembly election under STV in 1973. It produced a 70 per cent turnout and only 2.3 per cent spoilt ballot papers. Significantly, in every constituency, the voters elected representatives from both sides of the community. This has been a key factor why STV has been regarded as particularly essential for over 40 years in Northern Ireland's divided communities. It should also be noted that one unsung benefit of STV in Northern Ireland's local government elections has been the cross-community co-operation in a number of local authorities. The latest example of the introduction of STV elections is that of the Scottish local elections in 2007, repeated in 2012. With polling at the first election taking place at the same time as the election for the Scottish Parliament it was significant that voters found it easier to cope with an STV ballot than that for the additional member system used for the Scottish Parliament. There were only 1.85 per cent spoilt papers for the former and 3.5 per cent for the latter.

Given that, in local government in England and Wales, a majority of the electoral wards already elect three councillors for four-year terms, with each of the seats coming up by rota in turn for election, it would be relatively simple to follow Scotland and to introduce STV for English and Welsh local government elections. It would only be necessary to change from annual elections for a single seat to all-in/ all-out elections every four years. No protracted boundary change processes would be needed where multiple seat wards already exist.

STV has in fact already been used for elections to the House of Commons as it was the system used for the multi-member university seats from 1918 until 1945 when the anomalous system that gave graduates a second vote was abolished.

By-elections are rather like an adventure playground for electors and parties alike and provide an opportunity for the public to express its views on the party in power.[24] Occasionally they are used by sitting MPs to test the views of their constituents on an issue of principle.[25] Under party list PR systems it is not feasible to hold a by-election for a casual vacancy caused by a member elected on the list. In such cases, as in Scotland, Wales, Greater London and for the European Parliament, the vacancy is filled, in effect, by the next candidate of the same party on the list.

Under STV there are two alternatives used in different administrations: either the original vote is re-counted and the former member's preferences distributed, as in Ireland, or a by-election is held across the whole constituency by STV – or AV in an election for a single seat – as in Scottish local government.

---

24 The Conservatives loss of Orpington to the Liberals (14 March 1962) demonstrated the deep unpopularity of the government and provided evidence of the potential Liberal revival; similarly Labour's loss of the mining seat of Ashfield (28 April 1977) was a vivid shock to the Labour government.

25 Conservative MP David Davis resigned his Haltemprice and Howden seat as a protest against the erosion of civil liberties. He was re-elected on 11 July 2008; two Conservative MPs, Douglas Carswell and Mark Reckless, resigned their seats when they joined UKIP and were re-elected at by-elections in October and November 2014.

POLITICAL CONSEQUENCES

OPPOSITION TO ELECTORAL REFORM IS sometimes linked to antipathy to coalition government. However, as we saw following the 2010 election, FPTP can produce coalition government and, of course, coalition is not inevitable under PR election systems. Sweden, Portugal and Spain, for instance, have had single-party majority governments under different PR systems and a number of other countries have happily survived with single-party minority governments. Also, in Scotland in 2007, with STV, the country's largest local authority, Glasgow, returned a majority of Labour councillors. However, PR does mean that to achieve an overall majority, a single party must be sufficiently popular to poll more than 50 per cent of the votes cast.

A party that harps on about the problems of coalition thereby indicates an acceptance of its immutable unpopularity and a permanent inability to achieve a majority of votes cast. In any case, opinion poll evidence suggests that a large majority of the public believe that: 'we should never have governments elected by less than half those who vote.'[1]

There is, first, a question of principle in that arguably a government ought to command parliamentary support representing more than 50 per cent of the votes cast. Second, does a Labour supporter deem it

---

1 Democratic Audit has studied polling evidence on public opinion on representation since the 1970s. See: http://blogs.lse.ac.uk/politicsandpolicy/no-clear-evidence-of-public-support-for-pr

worth inflicting 18 years of the Conservatives in government on the people, or does a Conservative willingly inflict 13 years of Labour in sole power on the country, in the selfish hope that some day each will again be able to exercise the same untrammelled power? This is, of course, what happened between 1979 and 2010.

Much is made of the issue of clarity for the voter. Parties formulate manifestos; the electors vote for parties; the leading party forms a government and implements its manifesto. The truth is very different. Most politicians adore manifestos but electors cast their votes for a multiplicity of reasons, probably the least of which is the manifesto. Image, instinct, class, leadership, a desire for change, or a single over-riding policy, all influence voters far more than the manifesto per se. In any case each manifesto is itself a package, the contents of which have been fought over – and traded off – by the leading politicians in each party. If they have found it difficult to agree every dot and comma, why should they expect it to be acceptable in detail to the electorate?

World events highlight the serious problem of the detailed election manifesto. No manifesto could have foreseen the transformation of east-west policy brought about by the advent of Gorbachev in the Soviet Union in 1989, or the effect on policy towards South Africa caused by FW de Klerk's speech in February 1989. Who could have foreseen the Gulf War when preparing the 1987 election manifesto, and, perhaps, most significant of all, no party included a commitment to deposing Sadam Hussein in its 2001 manifesto? A belief in the need to adhere to a manifesto in detail despite changing circumstances, rather than in a broader vision of changing society, is unhealthy in itself. It is worth noting that the poll tax was in the 1987 Conservative manifesto and much good the mandate argument did Mrs Thatcher or her party when the whole sorry mess unfolded.

The nature of coalition is often depicted in over-lurid terms by those who still want the chance of gaining complete power under FPTP. As we saw vividly after the 2010 election in the over-urgent formulation of the coalition agreement[2] it in fact operates more by negotiation on issues than by adopting the lowest common denominator. In other words parties regularly do deals on the implementation of programmes or of items promoted by one party, rather than re-debating and watering down policy. Inevitably there has to be joint agreement on a few items of commanding importance but these are precisely the kind of national or international issues on which a government ought to have majority public support. With STV, voters can indicate by their choice of candidates advocates identified with major policies, which items these are. With a coalition, much depends on whether the parties involved are prepared to make it work or are seeking ways of undermining it. Despite its considerable hassles and struggles, the Conservative-Liberal Democrat coalition found ways of handling the key issues and clearly demonstrated its commitment to completing a full five year term, as indeed it did, despite considerable strains and stresses. In the early governance of a devolved Scotland the Labour-Liberal Democrat coalition coped positively over two full terms – eight years in all – despite the inevitable tensions apparent from time to time. Both attitudes have been present in local government where there has been an increasing number of hung or balanced councils.

It is argued that it is undemocratic for parties to negotiate privately to form a coalition on which the electorate has had no opportunity to express a view. This holds weight only in proportion to one's determination to exercise party hegemony rather than to enhance political pluralism. If a politician sees office only in mandate-implementing terms, with total power to be exercised for the length of a whole parliament, plus the right to manipulate the political processes – including appointments and the date of the election – for party advantage, then he or she is unlikely to be much enamoured of coalition.

---

2   *The Coalition: Our Programme for Government*, 2010, can be downloaded from the website: https://www.gov.uk/government/publications/the-coalition-documentation

If, however, one sees power as being granted by the electorate for a specified time during which the legislature, as opposed to the executive, has important rights, so that those out of office are encouraged to promote their opinions, then coalition is seen in a much more positive light. In particular, the prospect of working with MPs from other parties can be seen as constructive rather than obstructive.

In any case, we always have coalition government. The issue is only whether it is an internal coalition or an external one. As noted above, FPTP tends to produce large broad church parties which are coalitions of widely differing views that often coexist very uncomfortably under the same party umbrella. Who, studying political history, could avoid noting how often individuals struggled to maintain a common front in public whilst having furious differences behind the scenes? The Whig and Radical affiliations in the Gladstonian Liberal party, the problems between Asquith and Lloyd George, Herbert Samuel and John Simon, Hugh Gaitskell and Nye Bevan, Michael Heseltine and Margaret Thatcher, are all examples of broad church problems even amongst leaders, never mind the backbenchers. In some cases, the protagonists did find themselves eventually in separate parties but all tried to be part of the internal coalition that FPTP requires from those seeking power. It is arguably much more satisfactory to have external coalitions which reflect the reality of political affiliation.

It is also the case with a PR system that parties often indicate their preferred coalition partners. In Germany for many years, for instance, the Free Democrat party (FDP) campaigned for votes for itself in its own right and also for support to continue or to change its coalition partner after the election. The FDP did on one occasion switch partners during a parliament. By so doing it incurred considerable adverse criticism and lost a significant amount of support. Later German coalitions included the Green party rather than the FDP. The electors are often very shrewd in their decisions via the ballot box! Even in Germany it is not always one of the smaller parties that has been in coalition government. Recently, for the second time since the 1939-45 war, a Grand Coalition of the two major parties was formed between right and left – the CDU and the SPD. The criticism that used to be heard, that the FDP was always in government and thus wielded more influence than its relatively small vote justified, was dealt with by the electorate, not least by being voted out of the Federal Parliament completely at the last election.

Whether or not a smaller party ends up in government for a disproportionate amount of time depends, of course, on the future line up of parties and on their electoral support. If that party abuses its influence it will inevitably lose electoral support. The possible entrenchment of third (or fourth) parties has to be measured against two important points. First, where it happens, it usually means that the third party is unlikely to become the first or second party, thus ensuring that the major influence continues to lie within the two larger parties. Germany is a prime example of this rule. Second, until 2010, FPTP kept virtually all MPs except those from Labour and Conservative parties out of government for 67 years. In Britain until 2010, it meant the exclusion from office of any politician, however talented, from the Liberal and Liberal Democrat parties. Britain needs to make use of all politicians of ability. I am not at all arguing for a 'national government of all the talents,' but rather for a democratic process that has the potential to use MPs from all parties in varying coalitions.

Finally, an argument often used against PR is that it facilitates the election of extremists when they have, usually temporarily, had some support, such as the BNP at one time. Taking the argument at face value it suggests that mainstream politicians are incapable of countering the arguments of extremists and must therefore stick to a system that keeps them out artificially. This, with its attendant tactic of not giving extremists a platform, and demonstrating against their participation in office when they are elected, is wholly counterproductive. A significant proportion of those who were sympathetic to voting BNP, or, more significantly today, UKIP, are those who feel excluded from the main currents of social life; they are often unemployed and live in areas that are vulnerable to street crime and clearly suffer from a lack of attention from public services. They are unlikely to vote at all without such fringe parties fielding candidates and articulating their frustrations, often blaming them on immigrants. For the so-called liberal establishment, including the churches, to attack UKIP only from a negative position serves only to reinforce their supporters' views and to risk making martyrs of their representatives. The only way to deal with extremism is to expose the fragility and the lack of factual foundation of its arguments plus its inherent and dangerous nationalism.

Until its decline in 2010 and thereafter, more than 50 BNP councillors were elected in Britain under FPTP – so the electoral system is hardly invulnerable to extremism. Significantly, the two BNP European MPs elected at the 2009 election were successful under a list system that enabled them to win with less than 10 per cent of the vote in their regions. Such are the vagaries of extremist parties that both lost in 2014. However, under STV the quota for election in the constituencies envisaged would be significantly higher and would be far less likely to enable extremist candidates to succeed. However, if a party, however extreme, can poll significantly, it must be dealt with politically rather than by an electoral fix. As Jean-Pierre Cot, French MEP and former leader of the Socialist group of MEPs, commented: 'You do not cure a fever by breaking the thermometer.'[3]

---

3   Quoted in *Chartist*, July/August 2009.

CONCLUSION

D ESPITE THE EVIDENCE OF RECENT elections that Britain has at least a three party system in which the relationship of seats to votes is so capricious as to call into question the legitimacy of the electoral process, it is possible that FPTP might still survive – even despite the 2015 election in which six parties polled over a million votes. It became a lottery election but, despite the widest political consensus since the days of the National Government some 85 years ago that the present system is deeply flawed, its opponents need to agree on an alternative if they are to succeed in replacing FPTP. To believe that the question of the preferred alternative can somehow be put on one side, whilst the principle of change is agreed, is politically dangerous and tactically flawed. This lack of a plausible alternative has always played into the hands of the supporters of the existing system.

The main reason why hitherto there has not been agreement on the preferred alternative is that too much attention has been paid to a somewhat ethereal search for the perfect system instead of considering the criteria for the optimum electoral system. The persistent tinkering with the NHS, believing that each reform will produce the perfect answer to its deep-seated and continuous problems, demonstrates what happens when there is no broad consensus on a workable alternative structure. Similarly, the example of local government finance provides a vivid example of the dangers of seeking a perfect solution. The Conservative government, recognising the opposition to local rates, leapt to embrace Mrs Thatcher's poll tax chimera with disastrous consequences. In terms of her government's survival, the holy grail turned out to be a poisoned chalice. Likewise the search for the perfect electoral system, which led Roy Jenkins to the Alternative Vote Plus, and a dead end politically, is, to change the metaphor, a wild goose chase. The Electoral Reform Society has examined every new electoral system proposal over its 125-year existence and has remained convinced that STV is in all circumstances the optimum system. It has fine-tuned the counting procedures, particularly with the advent of computers, but the basic preferential system remains the same.

Too much emphasis is placed by politicians on the one requirement, that of party proportionality, without considering carefully the potentially detrimental effects on other important criteria of systems required to achieve pure party proportionality. Accountability, equal value and effective choice are each important and every electoral system must be considered in the light of all these criteria. No system with single-member seats can deliver sufficient proportionality; no party list can give accountability; and no hybrid additional member system can offer equal value.

In what is probably a genuine effort on the part of many leading politicians to meet the huge increase in public disillusion with politicians in general by looking at fundamental political changes, it would be catastrophic if they opted for a reform which further entrenched party influence and which singularly failed to address the electorate's wish – to be able to vote for or against individual MPs up for re-election without having to vote for or against their parties.

Only STV satisfies sufficient elements of the basic criteria and meets the current popular demands. Above all, because it empowers the voter in a unique way, it gives the electorate effective choice. Not only is it the best system, it also offers by far the best political opportunity for uniting the opponents of FPTP and the progressive movement for change. Of all the alternatives to the present system, STV best stands up to cross examination.

APPENDIX 1:

SYSTEMS IN USE IN THE UK

European Parliament:
England, Scotland and Wales: Closed regional lists; proportional voting only for party (or independent), not for candidate.
Northern Ireland: Single Transferable Vote; One constituency, three members.

United Kingdom Parliament:
Single member constituencies: First-Past-the-Post.

Scottish Parliament:
Additional Member System: 73 elected under First-Past-the-Post; 56 elected in eight regions to make the overall result proportional.

Welsh Assembly:
Additional Member System: 40 elected under First-Past-the-Post; 20 elected in five regions to make the overall result proportional.

Northern Ireland Assembly:
Single Transferable Vote: 18 constituencies each electing six members.

England and Wales local government:
First-Past-the-Post.

Scottish local government:
Single Transferable Vote.

Northern Ireland local government:
Single Transferable Vote.

London Assembly:
Additional Member System: 14 elected under First-Past-the-Post; 11 elected from a single list to make overall result proportional.

Police and Crime Commissioners:
Supplementary Vote: First and second preferences marked; if no candidate has overall majority, third place and below candidates are excluded and their second preferences, where indicated, are then distributed where they are for the first or second placed candidate.